Divine Love—
from Soul Mate Lessons
to Twin Flame Reunion

INGRID DARRAGH

BALBOA.
PRESS

A DIVISION OF HAY HOUSE

Balboa Press books may be ordered through booksellers or by contacting:

Balboa Press
A Division of Hay House
1663 Liberty Drive
Bloomington, IN 47403
www.balboapress.com
1 (877) 407-4847

Because of the dynamic nature of the Internet, any web addresses or links contained in this book may have changed since publication and may no longer be valid. The views expressed in this work are solely those of the author and do not necessarily reflect the views of the publisher, and the publisher hereby disclaims any responsibility for them.

The author of this book does not dispense medical advice or prescribe the use of any technique as a form of treatment for physical, emotional, or medical problems without the advice of a physician, either directly or indirectly. The intent of the author is only to offer information of a general nature to help you in your quest for emotional and spiritual well-being. In the event you use any of the information in this book for yourself, which is your constitutional right, the author and the publisher assume no responsibility for your actions.

Any people depicted in stock imagery provided by Thinkstock are models, and such images are being used for illustrative purposes only. Certain stock imagery © Thinkstock.

Print information available on the last page.

ISBN: 978-1-4525-9246-6 (sc)
ISBN: 978-1-4525-9247-3 (e)

Balboa Press rev. date: 09/09/2015

Praise for *Divine Love – from Soulmate lessons to Twin Flame reunion*

"Are you ready to remember and say yes to what really matters? In this beautiful book Ingrid guides and supports you to process, heal and transform past hurts and to connect more deeply with the Self and the ever present divine love for yourself, the one you are meant to be with and others. She offers lots of tools and insights to use on your journey and inspires you with her own story, authenticity and commitment."

Duncan Coppock, Author of "The Self Factor - The power of being you"

"There is no subject more important to us than Love. Ingrid skilfully guides the reader through the challenges to real love in its aspects of divine love, self-love, and loving relationship - offering wisdom gleaned from her own journey and years of coaching others. May this book become a precious friend on your own journey."

Miranda Macpherson, Spiritual Teacher, Counsellor & Author of "Boundless Love"

"We are all spiritual beings living through and experiencing a human life, which is a work in progress. In this book, Ingrid helps the reader to develop inner confidence and self-love, to attract more loving people into your life and to be ready for a lasting, loving and mutually supportive 'special' relationship. Create your 'happy ever after'- fill it with love and make it fabulous!"

Chrissie Astell, Author & Spiritual Educator

"Love is simple. We humans have overcomplicated this most precious of gifts. In this "Divine Love" book, Ingrid eloquently answers some of the age-old questions about love that most people struggle to get to grips with. She helps the reader unravel the mystique and mysteries of love in a way that is practical and useful to where you are at now. If you are looking to create the most exquisite relationship that lasts, then this book is the key to your freedom - the freedom to be in the most amazing relationship that you can imagine."

Harun Rabbani, Author, Broadcaster and Creator of Soulmate Wisdom

"Ingrid lives and teaches at the highest level and "Divine Love" is such a gift to us, bringing together everything she has learned along her path. Her wisdom and power to uplift have been perfectly captured within these pages - it felt like I was receiving a download of energy as I was reading! If you are looking for a book to transform your love life and shake the patterns of the past, look no further. Let Ingrid be your wise and loving guide."

Julie-Anne Graham, Author/Illustrator of the children's picture book "The Perfect Percival Priggs"

To my father, Pat Darragh, my first experience of divine love in this lifetime. You are always in my heart and your spirit lovingly guides all that I do.

I would like to thank:

My father, Pat Darragh, for all of the love that you shared with your family and all whom you came into contact with during your time here on Earth. You are always in our hearts.

My mother, Viviane Darragh, for your love and support and for teaching me to be independent.

My son, Lewis, for bringing me back to life. For increasing the divine loving presence on this planet, simply by your existence. Thank you for choosing me to be your Mummy.

My true love – "I want to love you forever and a little bit longer." Now, I AM home.

My soul sister Patricia Lübeck, for your unending love and support to myself and also to Lewis. We are so blessed to have you in our lives.

All of my family and friends, in particular my sisters - Tanya, Nicole and Lauren, brothers in law Darren and Melvin, and nieces Holly and Eva - for your unconditional love and support, especially during the most challenging times in my life. It has meant so much to me.

All of my clients that have had 1to1's with me and / or attended my workshops - it has been an honour to share in your journey and to witness your growth thus far. Thanks in particular go to those that agreed to be case studies in this book, to help others with their learning and their growth. You are an inspiration and my greatest teachers.

My previous partners - thank you for the love that we shared, as well as the lessons.

My good friend Sonia Longridge - for your support, encouragement and mentoring, you hold a very special place in my heart. Also (the late) Bill Longridge, for your coaching and counselling to help me through the divorce and your friendship and loving support, as well as Bill's daughters, Kieran and Sharon, for allowing me to include Bill's Loving Qualities list in this book.

Duncan Coppock, my teacher at Coach U and my Mentor Coach through some very challenging and very dark days of the soul. For your loving support and inspirational coaching, which helped me to always look within, to be open to the learning and to return home to my Self.

Antera and Omaran, for having the courage to share your story of Twin Flame reunion to help and inspire others and for your commitment and dedication to your spiritual work here on earth.

My teachers, Louise L Hay, Dr Wayne Dyer, Esther and Jerry Hicks, Doreen Virtue, Marianne Williamson, Dr Gay & Dr Kathlyn Hendricks, Eckhart Tolle, Chrissie Astell, Diana Cooper – and many others. Your books and audios were my constant companions and my guiding light, especially during my darkest times. With gratitude for your wisdom and inspiration and for your commitment to supporting humanity to return to love.

My EFT Teacher, Heather Johnston, for your teaching and your friendship, I am very grateful.

My soul friend, Kathy Denver, for all your love and support over the years. I am honoured to have shared in your journey.

Lastly, but by no means least, to God, the Angels and my guides and helpers in the Spirit world. "Many are called". Thank you for your infinite divine love and patience with me, until I was ready to hear the call, and for your ongoing guidance and support. I am an instrument of your peace and thy will is my will.

Contents

Foreword xv

Introduction xix

Chapter 1   What is love? 1

Chapter 2   EFT Tapping 8

Chapter 3   Falling in love with your Self first 12

Chapter 4   Healing from relationship break ups 39

Chapter 5   What do you want and need in a partner? 55

Chapter 6   Using the law of attraction and other practical tips 71

Chapter 7   What is holding you back? 89

Chapter 8   The importance of forgiveness 100

Chapter 9   Soulmate vs. Twin Flame 118

Chapter 10   Preparing for Divine Love / Twin Flame reunion 136

Recommended reading & resources 161

About the Author 165

Foreword

I feel honoured and very grateful to Ingrid for inviting me to write a foreword for her book "Divine Love – from Soulmate Lessons to Twin Flame Reunion". This is an inclusive and accessible book that brings together the practical and spiritual tools that we all need - and can practice - for bringing real love into our lives in ways that are meaningful to us.

I am particularly delighted because teaching about Divine 'Love' and bringing the Christ Light message that *love is the most important aspect of life itself* is my passion too. And so to be able to contribute, in any small way, to Ingrid's work which has been so lovingly drawn together over eight full years, in a format that works to help other people learn from her experiences, so generously shared, resonates with my heart.

Our life's work is very similar. It is about helping others to connect with their soul's purpose in life. To love and be loved. Like Ingrid, my belief is that we are all *spiritual beings* living through and experiencing a *human* life. My own human life is a work in progress. Like Ingrid's (and indeed many others), it has been - and still is - extremely challenging at times. It has taken me a long time to feel loved and to really know that *we are always loved*. Loving is part of the human condition. My experience has shown that anyone trying to find their way through life without love is the hardest path of all. Science has now shown that if we live without it, we fail to thrive.

The way we have been brought up and the mixed messages we were perhaps given by teachers, parents and siblings in our early years, followed by hard knocks taken as young adults may have left us with the wrong impression of ourselves – that is to say, one of worthlessness. We may then go through adult life either: as hardened cynics - which destroys our soul, or we frantically rush around trying to please everyone - which is impossible and can wear us out (emotionally and physically). Either way, there is often a risk of criticising other people without real cause because we feel bad about our own failings, and worse, we can become dreadfully hard task masters. From within that negative space our hearts and souls are suffering. We crave love, but at the same time we are literally pushing it away.

So many of us have not yet learned that what we spend our time thinking about and giving energy to is exactly what we create in our life, which perpetuates the cycle. We then attract new and even more difficult relationships, which can only succeed in reinforcing our sense of lack. We experience the very deep human suffering of emotional pain and heartache that our negative self-talk has taught us to expect - without changing this pattern, we can even become ill.

We really just need to shift our conscious thinking a little at a time. We need to learn new techniques, a different way of being comfortable with, and kind to, our self. Taking care what you say to yourself is vital. How many times a day, for example, do you use words which are running yourself down? Or do you hear yourself repeating the same old epic life-story? We are the creators of our own destiny - with a great deal of Divine assistance - but what we 'put out there' is what the Universe helps us to make happen.

Using positive affirmations is one way of consciously changing what we say and how we say it and is a great tool for your kit bag. Ingrid shows you how to combine affirmations with other tried and tested techniques - that really do work!

It is important to point out that we should never be misled by the word 'love'. There is no implication of 'wimpishness' or softness here. Working and living in a loving way (or even communicating lovingly with angels) is not all 'happy-clappy, fluffy stuff'. Being kind in action and thoughtful and considerate of others in a loving way does not have to turn you into a doormat. Far from it - there is certainly nothing soft and feathery about the imagery of the Archangel Michael! In doing so, you will become stronger, more focused, confident, compassionate, self-reliant, connected, centred and authentic. Unconditional love is mothering without smothering, being of service without the need to control or dominate. Acting with love is human *and* angelic.

By inviting pure love into our lives, we ignite the Divine spark within us - that part of us that is linked with God and the angels. Imagine the joyful positive energy and enthusiasm generated when we light that spark and it grows into a flame of passion. A passion that is reflective and attractive. All we need is pureness of intention and the desire to change.

Every one of us is born with an immense capacity for compassion and love. Is it difficult for you to think of yourself as an aspect of the Divine? Think of a quality you deeply admire, one that you would attribute to an angel. Visualise that quality in the form of a flower bud and in your imagination place it deep within yourself, into your very core. Now look at the flower and admire it, appreciate its beauty, its delicate strength, its perfume and its perfection. Remember these qualities and recognise that you too have these attributes. Recognise that your soul is a spark of the Divine and that it contains perfection, just like the flower. Allow yourself to love your soul, with all of its angelic qualities.

When we love and are being loved it makes our soul sing. We are nourished and whole. We cannot exist without love in our lives. Loving is an expression of kindness, of communicating from the heart and of compassion. Loving others is often easy, but in order to love completely and unconditionally we must first learn to love ourselves (which we can find challenging to do). Learn to give that gift of love to yourself.

Following the exercises so carefully set out here, Ingrid will help you to develop this confidence and self-love. You will attract more and more loving people into your life, and be ready for developing a lasting, loving and mutually supportive 'special' relationship.

We can all learn to change the next chapter of our story, and certainly if we wish we can even create a 'happy ever after' ending. Fill it with love and make it fabulous!

With love and blessings in abundance,

Chrissie Astell
www.AngelLight.co.uk

Introduction

As someone who spent the first part of my adult life seeking and fulfilling goals and achieving, I approached the age of 30 with an overriding feeling of "there must be something else". It felt so empty and without meaning. The universe was indeed listening and my then relationship ended and I found myself newly single at age 31 and facing a divorce, as well as serious health issues (a pituitary tumor and extreme PTSD) and a nervous breakdown. It was the first step on my path of awakening and my heart "cracked wide open" – with hindsight, it was all perfect and part of my training and apprenticeship as an Emotional Healer and Spiritual Coach and Teacher. I decided not to return to the corporate world, but instead set about healing myself, physically, emotionally, mentally and spiritually, which took several years.

The greatest challenges that I have faced in my life have also been my greatest teachers, with wonderful opportunities for learning and for spiritual growth. I was divinely guided to the books, courses and teachers that I needed at that time. I have to say that this was certainly not easy and if my "human self" had been given a choice as to whether to accept these lessons, my response would have been "No thanks, I am fine, just as I am". However, my Spirit would (and did!) accept them every time, because of the opportunities for accelerated learning and growth at a soul level, for that is what we are here on this earth to do, to learn and grow and awaken.

I have been blessed to connect with and work with wonderfully wise teachers, who have supported my awakening and growth. Once I was able to, I set up my private practice and began doing private 1to1 sessions with clients as well as group workshops, whilst also raising my son Lewis as a single parent. Somehow, I would find slots where I could journal, write and share my learning and insights along the way – in a monthly e-newsletter, or hand-outs to give to my clients and workshop attendees. I remember putting my son to bed when he was a baby and then taking some time to write in the evenings, (if I hadn't already fallen into bed exhausted from working and caring for him as a single parent). Or at other times, I would do some writing before a client arrived for their appointment. At times I wondered how I would ever find the time to write an actual book. (The PC that I was using was nearly 9 years old and would take half an hour to warm up, so I would turn it on and then go and do something else, while I waited for it to be ready for me to use!). But eventually, I would have enough material for a chapter and this would inspire me to keep going.

During this time I was also learning about love. It took me many years to heal from the breakup of my first soulmate relationship and the techniques that I learned and the forgiveness process that I developed as a result of these experiences are included in this book to support others as they learn and grow. Healing need not take years. In fact, ten years later at the age of 40, I was able to heal from a relationship breakup in a few months, by applying these techniques and doing the forgiveness process.

When I was asked by the publishers to choose an image for the cover of this book, I looked through the many that were available and the romantic images of couples together, walking along the beach, or hearts or sunsets just did not resonate with me. Then I came across one called "Gamma Ray Bursts" that I felt very drawn to. I looked this up to see what a Gamma Ray Burst was and here is what I discovered -

Gamma-ray bursts (GRBs) are flashes of gamma rays associated with extremely energetic explosions that have been observed in distant galaxies. They are said to be the brightest electromagnetic events known to occur in the universe and can last from ten milliseconds to several minutes. The initial burst is usually followed by a longer-lived "afterglow".

The sources of most of these GRBs are billions of light years away from Earth, implying that the explosions are both extremely energetic (a typical burst releases as much energy in a few seconds as the Sun will in its entire 10-billion-year lifetime) and extremely rare (a few per galaxy per million years). Very much like falling in love!

(Source: http://en.wikipedia.org/wiki/Gamma-ray_burst)

My intention for this book is to support you on your journey, so that you can access and experience divine love at deeper levels than you might otherwise experience and to support you to prepare to connect with your Twin Flame. You need not carry your own pain and emotional hurts and "baggage" around with you for the rest of your life – it is possible to heal the deepest hurts, betrayals and even traumas - to transform these, to see the lessons contained within them and to grow and awaken as a result of them.

In this book, I will share with you proven techniques to support you to:

- Boost your levels of self-love, by falling in love with yourself
- Become clear about what it is that you are looking for in a partner
- The importance of forgiveness and healing every past hurt
- Use the law of attraction and gratitude to help manifest divine love in your life
- Deal with anything that is blocking you from allowing divine love into your life
- Understand the difference between a soulmate connection and a twin flame relationship
- Learn how to embody the attributes of divine love and be ready to connect with your twin flame

Based on many years of coaching clients on a 1to1 basis and in group workshops, this book is filled with real life case studies and the valuable lessons inherent within them, as well as my own life experience, backed up by practical life coaching exercises and EFT tapping that you can do to attract the love that you deserve.

It is vital that you take the time to do these exercises and give them the time and attention that they deserve to develop new thought patterns, behaviors and ways of being. For instance, it is not enough to write out your new affirmations once in this book or your journal and think that you are done! It can take weeks and maybe even months of continuing to do these practices, to then see a real and lasting change in your day to day life.

It is important that we process and heal every past hurt, from all of our previous relationships, even going as far back as childhood. By completing the Forgiveness Process in this book, you can recognize the learning and personal growth that you have achieved from having these situation and / or people in your life and you can also release the associated "negative" energy, both emotionally and physically, to make way for more positive energy and experiences to enter your life.

It is equally important that we transcend our ego, or little self, to be ready to connect with this deeper divine love. As we transform the ego and become more mindful and self-aware, we no longer have any use for the separate ego state and we can then allow it to dissolve fully, as we become more enlightened.

Ultimately, we are here on this earth to learn about love and to deal with anything that is in the way of us experiencing divine love – the highest form of love possible.

I trust that you will connect with the lessons in this book that are relevant for you on your own journey. I have done each and every one of them myself (some of them many times) as well as recommending them to countless others. May they be a spark to ignite your own transformation and healing as you connect to your own source of divine love that is always present within you, for this is indeed your divine inheritance.

"The search for love is but the honest searching out of everything that interferes with love", A Course in Miracles.

Chapter 1

What is love?

"Love is the only reality and it is not a mere sentiment. It is the ultimate truth that lies at the heart of creation", Rabindranath Tagore

One of the main reasons that we are here on this earth is to experience and learn about love. Yet for many people, this can prove to be a life's work, an ongoing quest to find a partner to connect with physically, emotionally, mentally and spiritually, that they are compatible with and that shares their values and aspirations.

With divorce rates increasing, many people will go through more than one, or even numerous relationships, before they find this deeper connection that they are searching for.

In her book "A Little Light on the Spiritual Laws", Diana Cooper confirms that although we have our free will, there are also some pre-life decisions that our Higher Self made before we came to earth, with these soul choices being made based on the experiences that we need for our soul's progress. She describes it as being like "buying a round the world ticket. There are certain stopovers and pre-booked flights that you agree to before you set off." So if you have experienced the pain of more than one relationship break up or loss, you can take heart that this is in fact in line with your soul's path for this lifetime.

It is indeed possible that the pain of a relationship break up, divorce or bereavement can "open our heart" to a deeper level, which then connects us to a deeper level of our own soul. This then allows us to love at a much deeper level. I have certainly found this to be true in my own life. However, it is so important to process the strong emotions involved in a relationship break up or bereavement and heal these, so that we are not carrying that emotional baggage with us into the new relationship.

I will just mention here that it is mostly women that come to my workshops and for 1to1 coaching, so I have used wording in this book that assumes that it is mostly women that are reading it. However, for those men or for same sex couples that do read this book, please feel free to substitute alternative wording where required. Also, I have used the word God to represent divine source energy - if this does not resonate with you, please use whatever wording feels right to you. Please also note that the names of the people featured in the client case studies have all been changed, to protect their anonymity.

There are various definitions and types of love, however three common ones that are widely accepted are:

1) **Eros love**
2) **Philos love**
3) **Agape or Unconditional love**

1) <u>**Eros love**</u>

> Eros love is associated with romance and passion. It is based on the strong sense of attraction, can be driven by our most basic primal instincts and often occurs in the initial stages of a "romantic" relationship. Most of us will have experienced this type of love, often referred to as falling in love.

> It is often based on physical attraction and can be very absorbing. People will talk about the feeling of falling head

over heels, or being swept off their feet, experiencing feelings of ecstasy and bliss. These feelings of oneness and bliss during this period of "falling in love" are generally accepted to come to an end, some suggest that they will last between nine and eighteen months. The rush of excitement can recede and each person once again focuses on their own self and ego traits can resurface. It can be around this time that one or each partner will realise that this person that they feel so in love with is actually not perfect, which does not comply with the myth that people often grow up with, that there is one person out there in the world that is completely perfect and that being with them will be easy and effortless in every way. Many relationships come to an end around this time because of this.

In the real world however, being in a relationship can require effort from both parties, with both needing to be willing to address whatever is coming up, be it differing views on managing the finances, perhaps raising children together, how to spend free time together, career choices, what constitutes a healthy sex life, family obligations... the list is endless.

2) **Philos love**

Philos love is the type of love that we associate with close friends and family relationships, even work colleagues.

Associated with philos love is that it is based on friendship, deep caring, respect, trust, admiration, and loyalty.

It has been said that friendship can be seen as a firm foundation for a successful lasting relationship to develop. This allows time for trust and respect to be established, then stronger emotions to develop over a period of time.

Philos love is less erratic than Eros love and is more focused on giving and receiving, so it is a mutually beneficial situation.

Each person is partly focused on what he or she can get out of it, but they are also partly focused on what they can offer to their partner, so it is very much a two-way flow of giving and receiving, whereas Eros love can be more concerned with the "self", with each individual focusing on their own wants or needs as their first priority.

3)   Agape - unconditional love

The third and even higher type of love is known as "agape", or unconditional love. It would be fair to say that Agape love is a higher kind of love than Philos or Eros love, in that it requires greater levels of conscious awareness. It relates to our relationship with everyone and everything - our romantic partner, friends, family, even work colleagues. It is a love that is selfless, where a person will give love to another person even if this does not benefit them in any way, so they are not expecting something in return.

Agape love sees the highest good in everyone, despite the behaviour that he or she may be exhibiting at that time. It is kind, giving, compassionate and focused on the highest good.

It could be said that eros love is predominantly at a physical level, philos love is at the mental level, and agape love is at a spiritual level.

Agape love requires that we love the other person and want happiness for them without having strings attached, without wanting anything in return. Conditional love is where we love someone because we can get something from them, we love them because that person makes us feel good, or because they do things that we approve of or that we benefit from in some way. If we love in this conditional way, we make the other person a source (or the only source) of love for us, rather than drawing on the limitless well of love that we already have within. Agape or divine love is limitless and without conditions or strings being attached, without expectation on what we can get from the other person or how they can fulfil us and make us feel good within ourselves.

Agape love can be seen in the unconditional love that a parent has for their child, which is usually there from the moment that they are born. I certainly felt this for my child even from the moment of conception in the womb - I immediately made changes in my life regarding what I would eat, managing my stress levels and taking the recommended vitamin supplements so that I could give my baby the opportunity of a safe and healthy development period in the womb. Following two and a half days of labour, where my son took his time coming into the world, then an emergency caesarean section following complications, I finally got to see and hold my little one, after feeling his every movement for the previous nine months. This agape love has continued to grow and deepen over time. Even now, if we are out for the day and he becomes tired or irritable towards the end of the day out, I can see the underlying tiredness behind the behaviour and we talk about this together and I assure him that Mummy loves him, even when he is tired and grumpy. It amuses me when the shoe is on the other foot and he says the same thing back to me when I am tired and grumpy!

Agape love can also be seen when a child helps and supports their parent, or someone helps their partner, as they age or during a period of illness. This caring and giving is indeed selfless, with the carer focusing on their loved one and not expecting anything in return.

Developing this higher Agape love can take time and effort and can even be seen as an ongoing spiritual practice within a relationship. It is a healthy balance of giving and receiving, with healthy boundaries established in the relationship. Ideally, in a healthy intimate adult relationship, all of these types of love are present - eros (romantic love and physical attraction), philos (friendship and companionship) and agape (higher love).

The highest form of agape love is beyond what we typically experience as humans - the divine love that God has for us. This can be seen as our highest aspiration, to love ourselves and others as God loves.

> *"Immature love says: 'I love you because I need you.' Mature love says 'I need you because I love you.'"* - *Erich Fromm*

Spiritual Love

One of my favourite descriptions of this spiritual love that we are describing is in *1 Corinthians 13* -

> "If I speak in the tongues of men or of angels, but do not have love, I am only a resounding gong or a clanging cymbal. If I have the gift of prophecy and can fathom all mysteries and all knowledge, and if I have a faith that can move mountains, but do not have love, I am nothing.
>
> If I give all I possess to the poor and give over my body to hardship that I may boast, but do not have love, I gain nothing.
>
> Love is patient, love is kind. It does not envy, it does not boast, it is not proud. It does not dishonour others, it is not self-seeking, it is not easily angered, it keeps no record of wrongs.
>
> Love does not delight in evil but rejoices with the truth. It always protects, always trusts, always hopes, always perseveres.
>
> Love never fails. But where there are prophecies, they will cease; where there are tongues, they will be stilled; where there is knowledge, it will pass away.
>
> For we know in part and we prophesy in part, but when completeness comes, what is in part disappears.
>
> When I was a child, I talked like a child, I thought like a child, I reasoned like a child.

When I became a man, I put the ways of childhood behind me. For now we see only a reflection as in a mirror; then we shall see face to face.

Now I know in part; then I shall know fully, even as I am fully known.

And now these three remain: faith, hope and love. But the greatest of these is love".

In her book "The Wisdom of Florence Scovel Shinn", Shinn encourages us to pray for the *divine selection*, telling us that "Real love is selfless and free from fear. It pours itself out upon the object of its affection, without demanding anything in return. Its joy is in the joy of giving... Pure, unselfish love draws to itself its own; it does not need to seek or demand." She invites us to give this perfect selfless love and to salute the divinity in others. As we send out real love, it will return to us.

We will explore the attributes of divine love further later in this book.

"Love is a state of being. Your love is not outside: it is deep within you. You can never lose it, and it cannot leave you. It is not dependent on some other body, some external form." Eckhart Tolle

Chapter 2

EFT Tapping

EFT (Emotional Freedom Techniques) Tapping has been used from the 1970's onwards and was based on the body's energy meridians that are also used in other therapies such as acupuncture and reflexology. It has its roots in Thought Field Therapy (Roger Callahan), then Gary Craig developed EFT in the mid-nineties. Silvia Hartmann co-founded the Association for Meridian Energy Therapies (AMT) in 1998 and developed Energy EFT - which has become known as the "next generation of EFT". It is this Energy EFT technique that I am focusing on here - I am trained in both, but I like the simplicity of Energy EFT, or Heart and Soul EFT, as well as the fact that it begins and ends with focusing on the heart chakra, which brings in a beautiful energy and connection to the spiritual heart centre.

We will be using EFT tapping for many of the personal growth exercises in this book and I have added some videos with examples of EFT tapping to my website www.ingriddarragh.com and also my Facebook page "Ingrid Darragh - Divine Love."

Using Energy EFT Tapping

Energy EFT starts (and finishes) by putting both hands flat on the centre of the chest (the heart chakra) and taking three deep breaths in and out.

It uses 14 major meridian points, which generally are at the start or end of a major meridian.

These 14 points are:

- The top of the head
- The third eye (in the middle of the forehead)
- Eyebrow - at the inner beginning point of your eyebrow
- The outer corner of the eye
- Under the eye (directly under the pupil if you are looking straight ahead)
- Under the nose (in the middle of the fleshy part between your nose and upper lip)
- Under the mouth (in the middle of the indentation of your chin)
- Under the collarbone
- On the thumb, at the side of the nail bed
- Then at the side of the nail of each of your four fingers - index, middle, ring and little finger
- Finally, on the Karate Chop point, halfway down the side of your hand (below your little finger)

Then finish by putting both hands flat on the centre of the chest (the heart chakra) and taking three deep breaths in and out.

When you are tapping, tap lightly (as if you were touching a touch screen).

Tapping on these key points is thought to stimulate the flow of energy through the energy body, helping to release negativity and to support us to feel lighter, happier and more positive again.

You can think about something that you wish to focus on while tapping - then we begin by saying aloud something that is troubling us or keeping us feeling stuck. We then check in on the SUE scale

(Subjective Units of Experience), which is a scale from -10 to +10, with:

> -10 being the most upset, fearful, sad, depressed you could possibly be,

> +10 being the highest level of happiness, joy, even bliss, that is imaginable

-10 -9 -8 -7 -6 -5 -4 -3 -2 -1 0 +1 +2 +3 +4 +5 +6 +7 +8 +9 +10
Negative Emotions　　　　　　　　*Neutral*　　　　　　　*Positive Emotions*

(adapted from www.1-EFT.com)

It can help to allow your finger to slide over the scale and "feel" the score that feels right to you.

It is useful to check your score at the beginning of an EFT session, then check it again after a round of EFT tapping to see how it has changed.

Then, continue to do more rounds of EFT tapping to increase your score along the SUE scale towards a +10, ideally finishing on the +10 point.

We will use this EFT tapping technique for many of the exercises in this book, so please take a few moments to practice it and become familiar with it.

For more information on Energy EFT, please see "Energy EFT" by Dr S Hartmann, (DragonRising Publishing, 2012), or go to www.dragonrising.com.

I first came across EFT tapping in 2005. I remember coming across a book about EFT and I would often sit at my kitchen table tapping on myself to help manage my anxiety levels when I was going through a divorce and also when I was dealing with the symptoms of a pituitary tumor and PTSD (Post traumatic stress disorder). It helped me so much and I became a keen advocate of it and eventually went on to train as a Master EFT Practitioner, so that I would be able to use it with my clients.

I have witnessed such wonderful transformation using EFT with clients and also in my own life and within our family. My son even used it at age 5 to help with his nervous feelings when he was asked to represent his school at a poetry festival, which involved standing up on a stage in front of over 100 people. Not an easy task for a 5 year old to take on, but he was adamant that he wanted to do it. He sat in his car seat in the back seat of the car and started tapping on himself on the car journey to the festival. He just copied what he saw Mummy doing on herself at home at the kitchen table some mornings, as she said her affirmations and set her intentions for the day. It helped him to stay calm and to overcome his nerves. He did a great job and got a Highly Commended certificate for his efforts.

I highly recommend taking the time to familiarise yourself with the EFT tapping process, so that you can then use it on yourself. As EFT founder Gary Craig says, "Try it on everything!"

I am delighted that it is now becoming more well-known and that more and more people are using it and recognising the benefits. The success of Nick Ortner's bestselling book "The Tapping Solution" has really helped with this and his global event, the Tapping World Summit has helped to promote EFT on the global scale.

> *"When I first heard about using tapping or EFT (Emotional Freedom Technique), I thought it was delightful that something this simple and easy could really work. Tapping, just like affirmations, is another wonderful tool that can help us to let go of our limiting thoughts and negative programming from our past. And I do love the way the tapping process first releases the negative programming and then the affirmations help create more positive change and health in our lives."*
> Louise L Hay, http://www.healyourlife.com/blogs

Chapter 3

Falling in love with your Self first

"For many of us, love was conditional. It depended on how we looked, or how we threw the ball, or how we danced the ballet. Expectations were high, and we often failed to meet them. Later, this conditional love becomes internalised and we apply it to ourselves. We set impossibly high goals and feel bad most of the time because we have not met them. Love becomes a reward, something we give ourselves if we do well. True self-love is not conditional."
Dr Gay and Dr Kathlyn Hendricks

The first step towards embodying divine love is to cultivate and nurture divine love of the Self.

How good is your self-esteem?

Put very simply, your self-esteem is how well you think about yourself as compared to how you feel about other people around you, such as friends, family members, even work colleagues. Low self-esteem means that you think you are less important than other people, or that your needs are less important than theirs. This can be very subtle and may even be happening in ways that you are not even aware of. For instance, in my twenties, I regularly put my then husband first and would have prioritised something that was important to him over something that I needed or wanted. Similarly, in the workplace in the office where I worked, I often over delivered on what was being asked of me - this meant that over a period of time, even more was expected of me, so I continually had to raise the level of the quality and the quantity of work that I was delivering to be able to keep up with what was being expected of me. If someone had asked me whether I had good self-esteem and whether I loved myself, I would have said yes, of course I do. However, the ways in which I was treating myself and allowing others to treat me at this time of my life did not reflect this.

Low self-esteem can often begin to manifest in early childhood - you may have adopted this belief from the way that others behaved around you at this time - for instance you may have been abandoned by a parent, or a parent or sibling may not have acted in openly loving ways, so they were perhaps emotionally unavailable, or overly critical or even emotionally or physically abusive to you. You may therefore have learned that it is acceptable to be treated in unloving or disrespectful ways.

Low self-esteem can impact upon a person's behaviour in various ways. For instance, some people will be very timid and shy with low levels of confidence, feel that they are unworthy of having good things in their lives (including a loving partner) and can have a tendency to be self-critical and put themselves down a lot. They can also be likely to sabotage things in their life that do go well, as they feel that they do not deserve them.

Alternatively, others with low self-esteem may display aggressive or even violent behaviour, have a very pessimistic attitude, blame others for the things that do not go their way, gossip and put other people down to make themselves feel good, act in a self-righteous manner and may find it very hard to be vulnerable and show their true feelings or ask another person for help when it is needed.

When we increase our self-esteem or level of self-love to a high level, we then feel that we are "worthy" and are more likely to attract a loving partner who also has good levels of self-esteem and who will treat us respectfully and in loving ways. People with high levels of self-esteem are more likely to be kind, gentle, honest, respectful, responsible and trustworthy.

How much do you love your Self?

As we embark on our quest to find and connect with love, it can seem logical to focus on the other person - the one that we want to be with and to spend the rest of our life with - when in fact, the place that we need to look at first of all is our Self. We need to take some time out of our busy lives to look within.

Exercise- How much do you love your "self"?

Take a moment now to check in with yourself and ask yourself the following question- "On a scale of 0-10 (with 10 being the highest) - how much do you really love and accept yourself?" Be completely honest with yourself.

Write this down and put today's date beside it, so that you can monitor your progress as you go forward (if you do not have a notebook or journal, it would be worth getting one to use for the exercises within this book, as well as your observations and insights). Write down any words or phrases that come to mind as you do this, such as, "I am not as pretty as my sister", or "I would be attractive if I could only lose 20 pounds", or any of the negative associations that come to mind about your unworthiness, or whatever is in the way of you really loving and approving of yourself.

_____

Now, choose one of your negative statements and begin EFT tapping on it. Make a note of your score about this statement –

-10 -9 -8 -7 -6 -5 -4 -3 -2 -1 0 +1 +2 +3 +4 +5 +6 +7 +8 +9 +10
Negative Emotions   *Neutral*   *Positive Emotions*

(adapted from www.1-EFT.com)

Then do a round of EFT tapping using this statement.

Start by putting both hands flat on the centre of the chest (the heart chakra) and taking three deep breaths in and out, saying your statement out loud - for instance:

"I would be attractive if I could only lose 20 pounds",

Continue tapping on the 14 points, while saying this statement out loud, remembering to tap lightly:

- The top of the head
- The third eye (in the middle of the forehead)
- Eyebrow - at the inner beginning point of your eyebrow
- The outer corner of the eye
- Under the eye (directly under the pupil if you are looking straight ahead)
- Under the nose (in the middle of the fleshy part between your nose and upper lip)
- Under the mouth (in the middle of the indentation of your chin)
- Under the collarbone
- On the thumb, at the side of the nail bed
- Then at the side of the nail of each of your four fingers - index, middle, ring and little finger
- Finally, on the Karate Chop point, halfway down the side of your hand (below your little finger)

    Then finish by putting both hands flat on the centre of the chest (the heart chakra) and taking three deep breaths in and out.

Check in to see how you are feeling and what your score is now, has it changed? Make a note of this.

Do another round of EFT Tapping on how you are feeling now, using the words that come to mind, such as *"Well, I am actually very attractive just the way that I look now"*.

Check in to see how you are feeling after this second round of tapping - what your score is now, has it changed again? Make a note of this.

As your score moves along the SUE scale from the negative side to the neutral point to the plus side, the tapping releases the energy associated with the negative thoughts and emotions and brings us into balance and then allows the positive energy to flow with the positive thoughts and emotions that you tap on.

You could then focus on the things that you really love about yourself and do a full round of EFT Tapping on them, for instance *"I have a lovely smile and a kind heart"*, or *"I am a beautiful and sensual woman"*, or anything that comes to mind. (It is best to use your own words rather that someone else's words).

Notice how you feel in your body as you tap, paying attention to any sensations or feelings. Usually there is a lighter feeling that comes in, of letting go of the old thoughts and feelings.

Continue to tap - focus on what it would feel like to have amazing levels of self-belief and self-esteem, see and feel yourself living your best life, feeling totally fulfilled, happy and content. Do more rounds of EFT tapping to increase your score along the SUE scale towards a +10, ideally finishing on the +10 position.

I have to mention here that it is <u>absolutely necessary</u> to do the exercises that are contained within this book. It is important to be aware of and take responsibility for your previous love choices and behaviours that have led you to where you are at right now, knowing that your thoughts and behaviours can be changed and that you can develop a greater sense of self awareness and in effect, coach yourself towards a deeper experience of divine love in your life.

When I mention self-love, I do not mean in an arrogant or egotistical way. I mean having a healthy level of respect for yourself, as well as being loving and kind to yourself at all times.

When I first came across this concept of "loving myself" it was 2004, I was in my early thirties and going through a very challenging time in my life - I had separated from my husband and partner of 14 years (my childhood sweetheart) and my confidence was at an all-time low and I was also going through a serious illness. My scores were pretty low when I first asked myself this question - they were about a 4 out of 10.

I was also a people pleaser - I would go out of my way to please others and would go along with whatever they wanted, often sacrificing my own needs or priorities as I felt that their needs were more important than mine. With hindsight, I can see that I was setting myself up to attract in a partner that was used to taking more than they were giving, was used to acting in selfish ways, being the centre of attention and having their needs met without question or delay.

I realised that I had to set much stronger boundaries in all areas of my life, as I was also giving more than I should at work and in some of my friendships as well. Having strong and healthy boundaries is so important in our lives. This is where we let people know very clearly and assertively what behaviours are acceptable in our presence. We can focus on explaining what works for us and express this calmly and assertively. By using a calm and neutral tone of voice, we can do this in a kind and loving way.

For instance, I was once in a relationship with someone who would become very agitated and raise their voice when there was a point of conflict that we were discussing between us. When that occurred, I would calmly point out to them that I would appreciate it if they would lower their voice when they were discussing something with me and I would ask them to lower their voice while the discussion continued. If they continued to act in an aggressive manner, I would repeat my request and explain that if they were unable to meet my request and treat me with the manners and respect that I deserve, that I would leave the room and that we would then continue the discussion at another time when they were feeling calmer. I would then proceed to leave the room if that behaviour continued, as it was unacceptable to me. It was interesting to notice that as I became more assertive about how I wanted others to treat me, i.e. in a more respectful way, the people around me paid attention to this and treated me with more kindness, respect and manners.

As well as setting stronger boundaries in my life, I also made a commitment to work on my feelings of self-worth. I was studying for a Life Coaching qualification with Coach U in the States, which was perfect timing for me. I began using the affirmation: "I love and approve of myself" that I came across in Louise L Hay's book, "You Can Heal Your Life".

An **affirmation** is a declaration that something is true. You can choose a statement of something that you WANT to be true for you in the future and state it in the **present tense**. You can then repeat it to yourself over and over again, saying it aloud, writing it down - this repetitive action brings your affirmation into the <u>present</u> and can assist you in making it become a reality in your life today.

It is so important to learn to accept yourself completely and to love yourself unconditionally. Some of us will have a good level of self-worth, or self-esteem, others less so. Remember that this self-love can be developed and cultivated over a period of time. We are all unique - there is nobody else like you in the entire world with your gifts, experiences, personality, capabilities and life experiences. You are, in essence, a miracle!

Mirror work

One of the most powerful ways of doing affirmations is to **say them aloud whilst looking in a mirror**. Notice what comes up for you. Ask yourself - how much do I believe this, on a scale of 0 - 10? If it is a low score, you can be immediately aware of the resistance and can ask yourself why this is and work through it more quickly.

This is not about chastising or scolding yourself - simply notice where you are open and flowing and where you are resisting. It is important to be kind and loving to yourself at all times as you do this work. Remember that negative thoughts and patterns are only thoughts - and thoughts can be changed.

I used the "Ingrid, I love and approve of you" affirmation. I would say this affirmation aloud to myself regularly throughout the day - and in particular, I would stand in front of the mirror in the morning and in the evening as I prepared to start my day and as I ended my day. I would even stand in front of the mirror naked sometimes and say "Ingrid, I love and approve of you" - over and over again aloud to myself (there is nothing to hide behind when we are completely naked, we can feel exposed and at our most vulnerable).

If you have not already read it, I highly recommend that you get a copy of "You can heal your life" by Louise L Hay (Hay House), which is full of wonderful tips on affirmations, meditation exercises, relaxation tips, visualisation and mental imagery exercises. If you have already read it, make a point of reading it again - chances are there is a deeper message in there, just waiting to be discovered by you.

Exercise - Mirror Work

Choose a positive and loving affirmation for yourself now, such as: "_____ (your name), I love and approve of you", or something else that resonates with you - and write your affirmation here or into your journal.

Again, notice how true this feels for you, on a scale of 0-10 (with 10 being the highest) and write down your score along with today's date, so that you can monitor your progress as you go forward.

You can then check in once a week and make a note of your new score and the date as you go forward to see how your scores improve as you do this exercise (and the other exercises contained within this book).

You can of course do some EFT tapping on your positive affirmations, to "charge them up" and help them to feel more powerful as you speak them aloud.

Another tip is that you can write your affirmations on little cards and have them somewhere where you will see them regularly each day, such as on your bathroom mirror, on your desk, in your car etc., as a reminder to check in with yourself and repeat it regularly throughout the day.

Over time, your score will continue to increase and loving yourself will become part of your day to day life.

Case Study - Using Affirmations

One of my clients that has attended my workshops in Belfast and some 1to1 appointments is a beautiful young lady, we will call her Nadine. At the time of writing, Nadine was 26, relatively young in years, yet exuding such divine wisdom, reflecting how evolved her spirit has become in a relatively short timescale. Here is her story and her experience with using affirmations and manifestation tools to help prepare her for attracting divine love into her life:

"I have always been a big fan of the power of manifestation and the use of affirmations but I never truly understood their power until I started working with Ingrid. Through divine intervention, I won some group coaching sessions on how to "Design Your Ideal Life" with Ingrid just in time for Christmas in December 2009. As she introduced me to affirmations and encouraged me to look at my life on a deeper level and exactly what I wanted in life everything fell into place. I saw my job as a dark hole in my life, pulling me further away from my dreams with each passing day. After just one group session with Ingrid where I was encouraged to look at my ideal life I walked into work the following day, packed up my desk, told my boss "I quit" and walked out of the building free from the shackles of my fears. That afternoon I began promoting myself as a complimentary therapist and life took off. I stood daily looking into the mirror and affirmed "I love and approve of myself". Although very daunting at the beginning (and I have to admit I did feel very silly doing this), as time progressed, this simple daily practice of using affirmations changed my outlook on life. As my confidence grew, I began to meet challenges with strength. The more I worked on manifesting my dreams and loving myself, I got my dream job (as a holistic therapist in a nursing home) and also started my private practice. When I looked back over my manifestation list that I made with Ingrid at the beginning of 2010, I wrote at that time that I wanted to be employed as a Holistic Therapist within the health sector and that I also wanted to have a part time private practice where I could run workshops and teach therapies. And as I write this at the beginning of 2013, my dreams have come true.

I have now started working with Ingrid through the process of "Divine Love". What attracted me to this was that the coaching encourages us to look at ourselves on a very intimate level to fully understand our blocks to love, our unhealthy attachments to the past and our deepest fears, even those little ones that we find hard to admit (even to ourselves). After being badly hurt and emotionally scarred from a relationship which ended when I was 19 I have spent the past seven years fearful of getting close to anyone. My fears affected me in all relationships in life, not just those with a romantic partner. I found myself unable to trust people fully or allow them to get too close for fear that I would get hurt. With the coaching that I have received from Ingrid I have found healing on every level. I have cried, yelled, punched the life out of a bunch of pillows as I screamed every swear word ever spoken but this has all brought me one very valuable gift - the ability to let go of the past and to love myself at a deeper level.

As Ingrid taught me "You need to love yourself first, before you can love someone else." Although an easy concept to read on paper, putting this into practice was another story for me. All sorts of thoughts flowed - How can I love myself? Am I ready to allow someone into my life? Do I have the time and the space to attract someone into my life? When I sat with all of these questions and was completely truthful and honest with myself my answer to each question was a resounding No. My bedroom was still decorated the same as it was when my ex-partner (from seven years ago) lived with me. I lived in a space which constantly reminded me of the traumatic experiences of my past and every day trapped me further in an empty dark place of FEAR. Following a coaching session with Ingrid where I was encouraged to look at how welcoming my home was for another, I stripped my bedroom down to the plaster and sent every piece of the old furniture to the dump. As I stripped each piece of paper from the walls I stripped away the darkness of the past and sent all my fears to the dump with the furniture. Finally, I understood freedom.

I then created a sacred haven which reflects all parts of my personality. I surrounded this space with books, bright colours, positive sayings and fresh flowers. Each time I buy myself flowers my energy rises as I am doing something beautiful for myself. As I started to love myself more, I felt the energy of a new partner come closer to me and as I did my unresolved fears also arose - this time they were met with love rather than terror, with each fear lovingly being transformed into a blessing.

I continue daily with my affirmations and have created an affirmation tree for myself. I always make wishes and place them under a tree and in Mitch Albom's book "For One More Day" he speaks of his mother writing her wishes onto a tree and when asked why she does so she said "because trees spend all day looking up at God". My affirmations and my ideal partner list now hang from the branches of my tree, with my Rose Quartz and Rhodochrosite crystals.

I believe that with true spiritual life partners their two souls connect before their bodies do. I feel this process of "Divine Love" that Ingrid writes about here is truly sensational, as it has brought me into a deeper relationship with myself. I have worked through my very deepest fears which, if left ignored, would have continued to destroy my life as they had been doing. I have witnessed how this process has brought the most wonderful couples to find each other. Manifestation and Affirmations do work. I am living proof of it for I can now say with all my heart that I love all that I am and all that I have. Each day that I wake is a true blessing. I am so grateful to Ingrid for her encouragement, her love and her support - she is my healer, my inspiration and most importantly, my friend".

Note - Not everyone will be ready to make the kind of leaps that Nadine did, with feeling ready to leave her job right away, or to decide to throw out all of her old furniture, but she certainly felt ready to do so and she made great shifts in a relatively short period of time by acting on her intuition. You may feel ready to make similar leaps as you work through this book, or you may choose to take smaller steps, it will depend on what you feel ready for.

Exercise - Being your own best friend

It is also useful to check in regularly to see how kind we are being towards ourselves. We all have our inner voice, or "self-talk" running in the background as we go about our day.

Notice what tone of voice you are using- is it kind and loving, or is it harsh and judgemental?

Would you say those things in that tone of voice to your best friend? Or a young child? Chances are, you would not.

Take some time to notice what you are saying to yourself today and over the next few days via your own "self-talk" and make your notes here and the date:

_____
_____
_____
_____
_____
_____
_____
_____
_____
_____
_____
_____
_____
_____

We can often be our own worst critic - we would not dream of saying unkind or unloving things to someone that you loved and adored, so why would you say such things to yourself?

Remember, you can <u>choose</u> to change your self-talk if it is anything less than loving and kind. Make a commitment to be extra kind, gentle and loving to yourself at all times, especially when you are experiencing a challenging situation in your life. Love and support yourself with loving words and actions - what would a loving best friend say and do for you during a challenging time? Develop and nurture in yourself the ability to be your own best friend.

CHOOSE to love and support yourself at all times by putting <u>your</u> needs first and being there for yourself <u>unconditionally</u>, during the good times and during the more difficult times.

Take a moment now to reflect - how would a loving, generous, caring friend treat you when you are going through a challenging situation?

What would they say to you? What would they do to support you through this challenge? Write these things down here.

Make a commitment to say and do these things for yourself during any challenging situations and this will boost your ability to love yourself - unconditionally. With practice, this will become a habit that you do for yourself more and more. Your "self-talk" or inner voice will be so much more loving, supportive and kind as your levels of self-love and self-acceptance continue to grow.

"Learning to love yourself is the key to improving your life"
Patricia Cota-Robles, www.eraofpeace.org

Having had a period of serious illness in my own life in my early thirties, I was given the perfect opportunity to learn about self-care and self-love. Following a separation and subsequent divorce as well as many stressful years in the corporate world, working long hours and in a high adrenaline environment, I was diagnosed with a pituitary adenoma, a tumour or growth on the pituitary gland at the base of the brain. It went undiagnosed for many years, as the symptoms are unusual and the condition is not very common.

The pituitary gland is often referred to as the "master gland" of the human body - it controls most of the body's endocrine functions via the secretion of various hormones into the circulatory system. One of the main symptoms of this was that I would feel exhausted every day. The way that I used to explain it to people was to imagine that you had gone a few nights without sleep, then you ran a marathon with a hangover. That is the level of extreme exhaustion that I felt on a daily basis.

Often, I could barely get out of bed. A good day was being able to shower and then rest again, or perhaps have a short walk. It was a complete turnaround for someone who was so used to being independent and "in charge" of things, managing multi-million pound projects in the corporate world. This illness went on for many years. I did not require surgery, but was able to be treated with medication to manage the hormone levels, which helped to some extent with the symptoms. I was told that it was very likely that I would have to take this medication for the rest of my life.

Various psychiatric manifestations have also been associated with pituitary disorders, such as depression, anxiety, apathy, emotional instability, being easily upset and even hostility. I used to joke that it felt like being a combination of a pregnant woman and a teenage boy merged into one!

I decided to use this situation as an opportunity to learn as much as I could about physical, mental and emotional wellbeing and healing, so that I could improve my quality of life and manage the symptoms. I began listening to meditation CDs and learned Reiki, so that I could do a treatment on myself every day and I also read many books on self-development and healing. Over time, I found that my energy levels improved and I was eventually able to do courses and qualifications that would support me on my path to wellness - including: Life Coaching, EFT Tapping (Emotional Freedom Techniques), Reiki (and other energy healing systems), NLP (Neuro Linguistic Programming), as well as developing as a Psychic Medium and doing Angel Card Readings.

Over time, it became apparent that I also had Post Traumatic Stress Disorder (PTSD). PTSD is an anxiety disorder that can occur as a result of either being involved in or witnessing a major traumatic event. It is a common but often very misunderstood condition. The essential element of PTSD is that a person either <u>experienced</u> or <u>observed</u> an event which involved either <u>actual</u> or <u>threatened death or serious injury to either themself or someone else</u>. Any number of traumatic events can cause PTSD, including - serious accidents, natural disasters, violent attacks (e.g. mugging, rape, physical abuse, terrorists attacks or being held captive), or simply witnessing any of these events happen to another.

Symptoms associated with PTSD include:
1) Re-experiencing the event in varying sensory forms (flashbacks)
2) Hyper-arousal in the Autonomic Nervous System
3) Avoiding reminders associated with the trauma

If you think that you may have PTSD, please discuss this with your Doctor or a Therapist that is qualified to deal with it. You do not have to be a soldier on the "front line" to develop PTSD. I personally had extreme PTSD, twice over. The first time was as a result of being in a car accident (actual risk), the second was when I was told that I had a pituitary tumor (this time it was a perceived risk, as it was not fatal, but I did not know that at the time of the diagnosis).

I sought treatment for the PTSD as I felt very "stuck" and instinctively knew that I needed to resolve the root cause of the problem in order to "get my life back" as I saw it - to be able to be working again and have a relationship and perhaps a family one day and be able to cope with things that happened to me. Before I had treatment, I did not handle stressful situations very well and would have had problems with very high anxiety, whereas I knew that previously (before PTSD) I would have simply taken such situations in my stride.

The treatment that I had for the PTSD included Eye Movement Desensitisation and Reprocessing - (EMDR) - at the time, this was seen as a relatively new treatment for traumatic memories which involves elements of exposure therapy and cognitive behavioural therapy (CBT), combined with techniques (eye movements, hand taps, sounds) which create an alteration of attention back and forth. The effectiveness of this technique for single traumas is very high and results can be obtained in a short period of time. It needs to be done by a qualified and experienced EMDR Therapist. In my case, it seemed to "unlock" traumatic memories in my brain that had become "stuck". The part of my brain and the thoughts of being traumatised were then able to link up to the logical part of my brain, which knew that I am now safe and no longer in any danger.

I had about ten EMDR sessions altogether, which had a good success rate for me (although the Therapist did say that this was quicker than normal as I had already done some work on Anger Processing and Forgiveness, as outlined in this book, prior to going to see her).

Since having treatment, I have met other people who have had PTSD and some who still have it. I have found it interesting to note that people who have been in a physically or emotionally abusive relationship over a long period of time can also be very likely to develop PTSD. I have also noticed how people that have been through very high levels of trauma can come onto their Spiritual Path and develop and grow very quickly along this path. The trauma experience can open up their intuition and their "third eye" - leading them to a higher level of consciousness, sometimes clairvoyance and even a highly developed ability to visualize.

It is also important to point out that my spiritual growth and development during this time also very much contributed to my lower levels or anxiety, worry and stress. I learned Usui Reiki and did treatments on myself daily, I meditated and also regularly called the Angels and my Spirit Guides in when I needed them in various situations in my life. For instance, years later in 2008 while I was in labor with my son, I meditated and did Reiki in between the contractions and then called on Archangel Michael to protect me and my baby and consciously surrendered the outcome to God - so that when the Consultant told me that I would need an Emergency Caesarean, my response was that I trusted him to do whatever he needed to do to ensure a safe delivery of my son. My faith was rewarded as a very beautiful and healthy baby boy was born very soon after that.

These challenges that came into my life: a divorce, a serious illness and PTSD, also became the greatest blessings of my life, as they brought me onto my path as a spiritual life coach and healer. I learned and applied all of these techniques and principles to my own life to heal at a physical, emotional, mental and spiritual level, so that I could then go on to support other people with their healing journey. I also became extremely good at taking care of myself, being my own best friend and nurturing myself.

Affirmation - *I choose to see the <u>blessings</u> in everything that happens to me and to others.*

Exercise - Nurturing yourself

As well as becoming your own best friend, you can learn to become more loving and nurturing to yourself.

Make a list here of things that you love to do:

_____

_____

_____

_____

_____

_____

_____

_____

_____

_____

_____

_____

_____

_____

_____

_____

_____

_____

_____

When was the last time that you did these things? Are you taking the time to do them regularly, or are you allowing other things to get in the way and take a higher priority?

I wrote out my list of things that I love to do and then put it up on my fridge in my kitchen at home - every now and then I look over it and make sure that I am taking the time to do some of my favourite things - such as walking in nature, meditating, doing yoga, etc. and this helps to keep me balanced and energised to meet the day-to-day demands of running my business, seeing clients, writing, holding workshops and being a Mum.

Exercise - Building Your Energy

Another good exercise to nurture yourself is that you can check in each morning to see how your energy is feeling on a scale of 0-10.

Then, ask the question, "What do I need today?" or "What does my Soul need today?"

Ask yourself this regularly - in the morning as you get ready, or when you are having your breakfast, for instance. Write down whatever comes to mind and commit to doing that for yourself.

Sometimes when I do these exercises, I find that I need a walk in nature, a rest, time to meditate, to cook my favourite meal, or even some pampering such as a nice long bath, or polishing my nails... whatever my soul needs I commit to doing and I find that I feel very nourished, loved and fulfilled afterwards and that I then have higher energy levels and more to give and share with those around me, whether it be with my family or my clients. In fact, I regularly take a whole day to myself, so that I am rested and recharged to be able to work with my clients that are often going through very challenging situations in their lives and to ensure that I am also recharged in my personal life, with more love and energy to share with my son, my partner and those around me.

Remember - it is MOST important to be there for yourself when you are going through something challenging - let's face it, it is easy to be kind to ourselves when things are going the way that we want them to be going and life feels good at such times.

In accepting our self, it is so important to accept all aspects of our self - that is to say, loving ourselves, warts and all. Indeed, self-awareness is key - it is important to know and understand yourself, to love yourself completely, even your "shadow" self, or those parts of you that you would deem as being imperfect or less than whole. For instance, I can be very assertive or even bossy at times, telling those around me how I 'think' it should be done. I could choose to see this as a negative trait, but as a self-employed entrepreneur it is essential that I have a clear vision for my work, can prioritise my time and delegate where possible - all of which are positive attributes for a manager or entrepreneur to possess. To keep this in balance, I aim to keep this in check in my personal life by not always making all the decisions and going with the consensus of the family for our decision making, also to discuss fully with those around me as much as possible the choices that will affect us all. If I come out of balance in this or other areas of my life, those around me will lovingly point this out to me, sometimes bringing in a little joke, to help me to come back into balance again.

Case Study - Being there for and loving your Self

It is not always about finding a **_new_** partner, as one of my clients, we will call her Annalise, discovered when she came for some 1to1 appointments with me in 2011. Here is her story about how she connected with a deep level of self-love and self-acceptance:

"I was in a broken place - I had just walked away from a seven year relationship. He was a heavy drinker and after too many bad experiences for both of us, I decided that I just could not and did not want to take it anymore.

So I packed up and left him and our home in Spain and moved back to Belfast, with just two suitcases and two young children. I felt numb and broken. I gave myself permission to feel all of these raw emotions, which was overwhelming at times.

After living with my Mum for six weeks, I then moved into a new home and got the house and the kids sorted. I remember getting the girls to school one morning, then I got back into bed at 9am and just howled until 2pm before the school pick up again at 3pm. This release of emotion helped me to release my grief and to put what felt like a disaster behind me.

Over the next three months, I was just existing at times really and finding my way through it, giving myself time to breathe. I realised that I needed guidance and support so I called on Ingrid, who I had the pleasure of knowing through mutual friends.

During our first session together, Ingrid's calming energy helped to calmed me down, but I couldn't really talk about the pain without crying. For the first few sessions I had Reiki treatments, which was very intuitive of Ingrid, as I felt unable to articulate words just yet - I was still numb and feeling like I was in a dark place.

I remember holding onto the crystals that Ingrid gave me so tightly, carrying them everywhere that I went. I would feel calmer as I rubbed them during the day, as they were always in my pocket.

As I healed, Ingrid and I discussed many subjects in my 1to1s with her - my core beliefs, my intentions with the focus being on what I wanted. I remember Ingrid saying to me - "Check in with yourself each day and see what you need, what your soul needs that day, then make a commitment to do that for yourself". That was like a healing light bulb being turned on - checking in with what I wanted and needed was so delicious to me at that time.

In the further sessions that we had together, I felt lighter and brighter. Ingrid helped me through the process. I felt strong and focused for the first time in years. I came away feeling still somewhat delicate, but also stronger at my core.

I continued to allow my feelings to come up and I would have the occasional cry while listening to Adele's music, but sure who doesn't!

I remember starting to laugh again.

I believe that I would have still been stuck in anger and ego-based thoughts if I had not been supported and encouraged by Ingrid. I also surrounded myself with good people and supportive friends - I rebuilt my traumatic experience into a forgotten time, which feels so distant in my past now.

I was particularly amazed at how the EFT Tapping helped to release strong emotions and to raise my energy levels instantly. If I found myself driving and becoming upset, I would pull over and do some tapping for 5 minutes and I have to say, it is magic! I truly believe that the universe is magical and wants you to be happy.

Here I am, two years later - I got the happy ending that I so desired. I aimed high - I wanted a big love and I got it. My partner has not drank in two years - he fought to get his family back. After spending the first year living apart and attending counselling sessions together, we gently recreated our family and now I can honestly say that I have never been happier. I feel calm, loved, supported and our kids are so happy to see their Mummy and Daddy happy. Roll on the wedding in 2014 - we definitely got our happy ever after.

Our story shows that anything is possible and this was all helped by you Ingrid and all the skills that you have to teach others. You are a very special woman."

Exercise - Loving all the parts of your self

What parts of yourself do you find hard to love and accept about yourself? (Your "shadow" self?)

Make a list of them here and make a point to learn to love these aspects of yourself just as much as the other qualities that you find easier to love and accept.

Check in on the EFT SUE scale to see what score these feelings have, then do some EFT tapping on them to help to release the negative emotional charge around them.

Do some further EFT Tapping to bring your scores up to a positive number on the SUE scale, using words such as "Even though I am outspoken and even bossy at times, I love and accept myself", or whatever words come to mind.

Imagine yourself as a little child of three years old, displaying these attributes and acting them out, then imagine taking this child into your arms and telling him or her how much you love them.

Like attracts like

As you work on your own levels of self-love and boost your levels of self-esteem, you are more likely to attract a partner who also has good self-esteem and self-love and who will treat you in loving and kind ways.

As you learn to love and accept all aspects of yourself, you pave the path for others to love everything about you.

"In the realm of love, a paradox exists: you can effectively love others only when you can love yourself. If you cannot love yourself, you will try to fill the void of your own lack of self-love with the love of others. You will tend to demand from them what you cannot give yourself. …It makes you a bottomless pit; no matter how much love they give, it is never enough. The same problem exists if you try to give love to other people who do not love themselves. You will turn yourself inside out loving them, but it will not help. We all must learn to give ourselves the love that we want."
Dr Gay and Dr Kathlyn Hendricks

Chapter 4

Healing from relationship break ups

"Something very beautiful happens to people when their world has fallen apart: a humility, a nobility, a higher intelligence emerges at just the point when our knees hit the floor" Marianne Williamson

Some people fall in love and then go on to spend the rest of their life living "happily ever after" with that one person. However, for the rest of us, our journey will mean being with more than one partner before we find our happy ever after. Just as it can take a few (or even many) jobs in our lives before we gather up the learning and experience to go on to be promoted to the ideal job, doing work that we absolutely love, it can take a few (or many) relationships before we are ready to connect with divine love - to a love that is beyond our wildest dreams.

My first relationship break up came when I was in my early thirties, I had been with my childhood sweetheart for fourteen years and we had married and then found that we had grown apart. We decided to go our separate ways on the night before we were due to move into a beautiful new home, in a lovely part of Edinburgh in Scotland. As we were legally bound to go ahead with the move, this meant that we had to go through the process of moving all of our things into the new home, unpack, then put it back on the market to sell as soon as possible. It was a devastating experience at that time - it felt as though my right arm had been torn off. We then also had the experience of going through a legal separation and a subsequent divorce two years later.

Some ten years later, while working on completing the first draft of this book in February 2013, I found that the relationship that I was in at that time was coming to an end. I found myself in the position of writing about Divine Love while becoming single again! While there were many positive things about that relationship, there were also a lot of things that were not working out. I had an underlying feeling that something was missing and that the relationship would not last if we continued with it. I had to trust my vibes and take the difficult decision to separate.

I noticed that I felt very uncomfortable about putting my book "out there" while single, so I went for a long walk in nature to meditate, reflect on my feelings and speak with my guides and helpers in the spirit world. By the end of my walk, I realised that it was my Ego that wanted to give the impression of being happy and settled in a relationship when publishing my book, but if I kept all that I had experienced and learned to myself, I would only be helping one person (Me!), which would be very selfish. So I came out of my comfort zone and did it anyway. I took some time to process my feelings around the break up and did the exercises in this book to help me to heal and process the hurts and strong emotions associated with it, updating the book in the process to include more content and material about how to heal from a break up.

Break ups are rarely easy, but they do offer us an opportunity to understand at a deeper level how we have changed and grown as a person during the period of time that the relationship was in our lives, as well as to become clearer about what we are looking for in our next romantic partner.

"This world is a school and you have come here to learn...If you were right all the time, why would you need to come to school?" (Jesus), Paul Ferrini

Exercise: Post-relationship audit

It is a very useful exercise to become clear about what did and did not work for you during your previous relationships - this can help you to be more conscious of the aspects and the behaviours that you want to let go of, as well as to become very clear about the positive attributes that you do want to take forward with you into your next relationship.

This simple act of writing them all down helps you to become extremely clear and this can be particularly useful right after a break up, when you are feeling emotional, upset, even devastated - to focus instead on something that is rational.

Make your own list here about your previous relationship (or your current partner, if you are in a relationship at present):

What I like(d)	What I didn't/don't like

(Continue on a separate sheet if necessary)

The list of things that you did not like / did not work for you can also help to prevent you from being tempted to give in to the others person's pleas right after a break up, such as – "let's try again, it will be different this time", etc. Instead, you can focus on remembering why it did not work and make a <u>rational</u> decision on whether it would be worthwhile to look at reconciling with this person or to call it quits (more on this in Chapter 5, when we look at what you want and need in an ideal partner).

It is worth mentioning at this point that we often need to be careful just after a break up, as we are likely to be feeling vulnerable and there could still be an attraction, even if only at the physical level, with your ex-partner - meeting up to talk or have a coffee could mean that you feel drawn to spend time with this person that you were once so happy with - they may be willing to say all the things that you wanted to hear when you were together and it may mean putting more time, more energy and more love into something that is perhaps never going to work.

Be honest with yourself, look at your list of things that did not work and instead of meeting up with Mr Nearly-right, spend that time doing these exercises to work on preparing yourself for Mr Wonderful instead. Or, if your list of things that did work is a long one and there are only a few things that were not working for you, then by all means, meet with that person and talk about these areas and see if you both want to put in the time and effort to work on and improve these areas and give your relationship another chance.

> *"All experience happens for one purpose only: to expand your awareness...Your primary freedom lies in learning from the experiences that come your way. Of course, you can refuse to learn from your experiences. But this choice leads to suffering. If you don't know this yet, it won't be long before you do." (Jesus), Paul Ferrini*

Exercise - What have I learned from this?

Another exercise that can be helpful at this time is to reflect on what you have learned from having this person and this relationship in your life - about yourself, about the other person, about relationships in general -

Take some time now to reflect on your previous partners and the relationships that you shared - what were the main lessons that you learned as a result from having this person in your life?

Partner:	Lessons / learning:

(Continue on a separate sheet if necessary)

Trusting in the higher plan of your life

I believe that there is a divine plan for each of us that our soul agreed to before it incarnated here on earth - this includes what our main lessons would be during our time here and the situations that would come up on our path to help us to learn these lessons. For instance, you may have attracted a romantic partner who would be mean, controlling, even abusive in some way, because your soul had agreed that you were to learn about having strong boundaries, having good self-esteem, and standing up for yourself etc. Perhaps your life purpose would involve eventually helping, supporting, guiding and counselling others who had similar experiences to yours.

These main lessons will then show up in your life. It is important to look for the learning and the lesson that this person or situation is showing up to teach you. If you get the lesson and fully integrate it into your being, then it need not show up again. However, if you do not, then the lesson will show up again, either in a similar situation, with the same person, or with another situation or another person.

I remember when I was going through a break up and was feeling very sad and disappointed. I went for a walk in nature and as I walked I prayed and talked to God, the Angels and my Spirit Guides, as I often do while walking in nature. I confided in them about how I was feeling about the relationship break up. After a few moments, the reply that I received back was *"Have you forgotten that we know what we are doing?"* said with light-heartedness. It made me laugh and I immediately reconnected with my trust in God's plan for me.

I have learned to trust that if something (or someone) is for the highest good of all involved, it will happen. However, if it is not for the highest good, it won't.

By letting go of what you "want" to happen, you open up to the divine plan of everyone involved. You can then let go of the outcome and surrender this to God / source. There is always something even more wonderful planned for you at this level than you could even conceive of in your own human mind.

> *"Resistance is the decision to act alone.*
> *Surrender is the decision to act with God", (Jesus), Paul Ferrini*

Every situation that comes up in your life is an invitation to move closer to God, to become as God is, to act as God would act, to see others as God would see them and to treat yourself as God would treat you.

I also highly recommend doing the Forgiveness Process, as outlined in Chapter 8, to support you through a relationship break up (and all previous break-ups as well, to work through and heal the emotions that were and may still be associated with that relationship). This will help you to identify all of your emotions and feelings associated with the break up as well as to process them using the techniques that are outlined.

It is also of utmost importance to *be as kind and loving with yourself as possible* while healing from a relationship break up - go back over the exercises in Chapter 3 on monitoring your self-talk, doing your affirmations and mirror work and being your own best friend, if you feel that this is necessary.

Resist any urge to blame yourself or beat yourself up about the break up - remember that you were doing the best that you possibly could at that time - and so was your partner, with the knowledge and levels of awareness and consciousness that you both had at that time.

The following was sent to me on an email at a time when I was going through my first break up and subsequent divorce and I found that it really resonated with me, so I would like to share it with you -

Thoughts on Being "In between"

Affirmation: Today I will accept where I am as the ideal place for me to be.

If I am in-between I will strive for the faith that this place is not without purpose, that it is moving me forward, towards something good.

Sometimes to get from where we are to where we are going, we have to be willing to be in-between.

One of the hardest parts about being in-between, is that we must let go of what is old and familiar yet unwanted, (because we have grown beyond it) and at the same time, we need to be willing to stand with hands empty while we wait for God to fill them. This is the in-between place.

We may have many feelings going on when we are in-between - spurts of grief about what we have let go of, our loss. We may also feel anxiety, fear and apprehension about what's ahead, because it is unknown. These are normal feelings for the in-between place. Accept them. Feel them. Release them.

Being in between isn't fun, but it is necessary. It will not last forever.

It may feel as if we're standing still, but we're not. We're standing in the in-between place. It's how we get from here to there. It is not the destination. We're moving forward, even when we are in-between. Have faith. Trust yourself. Be extra specially caring of yourself during this time.

(Adapted from "The Language of Letting Go" by Melody Beattie)

> *"In the process of healing, you learn to give yourself the unconditional love you never received from your biological parents... in this process you are "born again", and re-parented, not by other authority figures, but by the Source of Love inside yourself... Slowly, you retrain yourself to value yourself as you are, here and now, without conditions. That is the work of each individual soul (how to love yourself)." (Jesus),*
> *Paul Ferrini*

Exercise - Lessons about love from childhood

This next exercise is useful to help us to discover what we observed and learned in childhood about love. This is in no way intended to blame our parents or caretakers- it is more to do with helping us to discover where our beliefs have come from (some of these can be at a very deep level, we may not even have taken the time to reflect on them and may not be conscious of them yet).

Below is a table with one column for Mum and one for Dad (If you did not grow up with both parents present, start with one and then label the other authority figure that you had in your childhood years, e.g. grandparent, step-parent, older sibling, etc.).

On each side, list 10-15 characteristics of that parent, such as cold, reserved, organised, smart, etc. and then do the same for the other one.

Mum	Dad
1.	1.
2.	2.
3.	3.
4.	4.
5.	5.
6.	6.
7.	7.
8.	8.
9.	9.
10.	10.
11.	11.
12.	12.

Mum	Dad
13.	13.
14.	14.
15.	15.

Look at this list and then notice where these people are generally opposites. Then circle or put a star next to the traits where they are very obvious opposites.

Then ask yourself the following questions:

1   Who was more fun to be with? Which one did you enjoy being with?
2   Who was more emotional? Who solved problems using their feelings?
3   Who used reason or logic more?
4   Who are you most like?
5   Who had the "power" in the household?
6   Who is considered more "successful"?

Make your notes here, in particular, who are you most like and who had the power in your household growing up:

Previous Romantic Partners

Now, take two of your main romantic partners (or more, use a separate sheet if necessary) that you have had relationships with and do the same for them:

Name:	Name:
1.	1.
2.	2.
3.	3.
4.	4.
5.	5.
6.	6.
7.	7.
8.	8.
9.	9.
10.	10.
11.	11.
12.	12.
13.	13.
14.	14.
15.	15.

Are there any similarities between the partners?

Are there similarities between a partner and one of your parents?

We draw to us people and situations based on our current beliefs. By making these beliefs conscious, we can shift them and then also shift the qualities of the people that we attract to us. When we become more conscious of our "love choices", we can then be aware of what we want to change going forward.

(Adapted from the book "From Doormat to Diva! Taking Centre Stage in Your Own Life"- Merci Meglino, Copyright 2003)

One lady who completed this exercise, we will call her Iris, had a real light bulb moment once she had finished it - she said aloud "I married a male version of my mother! Both my Mum and my ex-husband had similar attributes of being angry, moody, bossy, emotionally distant, serious, selfish, self-centred, controlling and judgemental! She was certainly the boss at home when we were all growing up - my gentle and kind father hardly got a say in anything. I am more like my Dad, so in my own relationships, I made an assumption (that I am only now becoming aware of), that my partners would be the ones to hold all of the power and authority and I would just have to go along with what they wanted, just like my Dad did with my Mum".

Psychologists tell us that people often go out into the world and fall in love with someone who has similar attributes to one of our parents - at a subconscious level, we associate love with what we experienced as a child growing up, so we go out into the world looking for that. This was certainly the case with Iris and once she became more conscious about her patterns and the behaviours that she wanted to change, she was then ready to be in a loving relationship that was a true partnership, with equal amounts of giving and receiving.

"Relationships exist to hasten our walk to God" Marianne Williamson

Challenging Outdated or Negative Beliefs

One lady who came to my workshops and for some 1to1 coaching, we shall call her Julie, was in her mid-thirties and was searching for her ideal partner after a recent break up. We began working through the Divine Love programme and she was doing the exercises contained within this book.

A very attractive lady, Julie was still frequenting the bars and night clubs with a friend that she used to enjoy going to, but she found that she was losing interest in this social scene and looking for a deeper level of connection with people. It was on one of these nights out that she met and felt very attracted to someone new. There was a very strong physical attracting and lots of flirting and she felt very disillusioned and disappointed when he did not call her after taking her number.

During our coaching session, we checked her score and found that her self-esteem and level of self-love felt like a 6 out of 10, which was a relatively low score.

We also reviewed what she did not like about the guy that she met (and also her previous partner) and the qualities that she would want her new Mr Wonderful to have instead, the results of which are below:

Mr Bad Boy	Mr Wonderful
Rude	Attentive
Aggressive	Affectionate
Disrespectful	Smart
Insulting	Witty
Inattentive	Playful
Unsupportive	Charismatic
Doesn't open up/show his feelings	Optimistic outlook
Scared to commit	Respectful of other people
Finds it hard to trust	Kind and thoughtful

Mr Bad Boy	Mr Wonderful
Needy	Interested in me and my interests
Jealous	Supportive
Stingy with money	Handsome
Selfish	Responsible- a man, not a boy
Drinks alot	Good father potential
Focused mainly on physical attraction / sex	Fun to be with
Wants to fit me in around his social life, friends	Open with his feelings
Wants to use me to enhance himself in some way	Passionate & sensual
	Willing to talk about his emotions
	Is there for me, no matter what
	Good manners
	Respectful
	Loving
	Sexy
	Can be comfortable and intimate together
	Wants to spend quality time with me
	Patient
	Healthy lifestyle
	Enhances my life, an even flow of giving and receiving
	Dependable and reliable
	Trustworthy
	Has good levels of integrity
	Honorable
	Reliable job, own home, own car, Financially stable

This simple act of writing down a list helped Julie to become very clear about what the difference is between Mr Bad Boy and what she was looking for in her Mr Wonderful.

We also discussed the concept that her Mr Wonderful could also be very flirtatious and fun to be with, both of which she wanted in her new partner, however he would also be extremely trustworthy and reliable and would only have eyes for her. During our coaching, she opened up to the fact that it did not have to be "all or nothing" thinking, that her new partner would either be Mr Bad Boy or Mr Completely Boring - she relaxed into the feeling of having a wonderful, trustworthy and reliable partner who would be fun and flirty with her, however, he would be completely respectful of this when out in public and when around other women so that she would always feel that she could trust him fully.

Cord Cutting

I first came across the concept of cord cutting in Doreen Virtue's Angel books and Angel cards. When we have fear-based attachments to a person or an object, we can form spiritual "cords" to keep the person or object from leaving or changing. These cords can be visible to those that are clairvoyant or be felt by those that are clairsentient.

They can be like hollow tubes and energy can flow back and forth between us and other people, such as family members, or previous romantic partners. As we sever or cut these cords, we can release the unhealthy aspects of these relationships, such as the part of the relationship that was based on fear or dependency.

We may not be aware of a cord being there, but if the other person is upset or feeling sad or they are needy and always expecting something from you, this can then feel draining, like they are draining your energy, which can lead to tiredness, or you may even feel their feelings of sadness, depression, anger, or whatever it is that they are feeling. If you are a healer or counsellor, you may even have cords attached to your clients or those that you teach.

It is therefore vital to cut these cords regularly, whenever you feel tired or drained and at the end of any client session or healing appointment.

- Simply take a few deep breaths and centre yourself in the present moment
- Call on whomever you pray to. You may also like to call on Archangel Michael to assist with this, as he carries a sword that can cut the negative aspects of the cords but leave any positive energy intact
- Now, send out the thought or say aloud – Please cut any cords that are draining my energy now
- Then wait and take slow deep breaths for a few minutes as you allow these cords to be cut
- You may be aware of physical sensations or just a knowingness that this is completed

The other person may even be aware that this is taking place and may feel the cords being cut and may even get in touch with you. At one of my workshops, we did this cord cutting exercise and an ex-partner got in touch at the exact time that we were cutting the cords. He sent me a message to ask me to get back together and to say that he still had feelings for me. However, I had worked through the exercises in this book and knew that the relationship was not right for me and was therefore able to respond with kindness to that effect.

> *"In the end these things matter most:*
> *How well did you love?*
> *How fully did you live?*
> *How deeply did you let go?"*
> *Gautama Buddha*

Chapter 5

What do you want and need in a partner?

In order to attract your amazing new partner to yourself, you need to become very clear about exactly what it is that you are looking for. If you wanted a new house, you would become clear about exactly what it is that you are looking for, for instance, what part of town you want to live in, how many bedrooms, parking, a garden, how many bathrooms, an older building or a new one - etc. You would then proceed on this basis, which focuses your attention on what you are searching for. So it is when you are looking for love.

I recall one lady at one of my workshops a few years back, she did not agree with this and so did not join in the exercise of writing down all the attributes that she wanted to attract in her new partner. When I bumped into her recently, she told me that she is still single.

One of my favourite summaries of loving qualities was the one that was shared with me by my late mentor and friend Bill Longridge, which clearly shows the loving qualities in the left column and their non-loving (opposite) behaviours in the right column:

Loving Qualities and Non-Loving Qualities in Friendships / Relationships

Loving Qualities	Non-Loving Qualities – the Opposite behaviours
Gentleness	Aggression towards others
Kindness	Physical or mental cruelty
Patience	Impatience / agitated attitudes
Unselfishness	Self-centredness
Generosity	Meanness of spirit
Tolerance	Intolerance of differences
Honesty	Dishonesty, deceit
Forgiveness	Unforgiveness
Sensitivity	Insensitivity towards others
Being real / authentic	Falseness and pretence
Celebrating all success	Envy of others
Allowing of Freedom / space	Overly controlling & possessive
Looks for the good in people and situations	Fault finding and critical
Compassionate	Attitude of indifference
Accepting of Others	Being rejecting / judgemental
Accepting of Self	Self-condemnation
Really listening	Inattention and disinterest
Forgiving own errors	Unforgiving of self
Can say "I'm sorry"	Inability to say sorry
Loyalty	Disloyalty
Flexibility	Black and white rigidity
Seeking to make amends	No attempts at finding a resolution
Appreciative	Taking things for granted

Treating others with dignity	Taking away another's dignity
Befriending & Nurturing	Being cold & unsupportive
Trustworthy	Untrustworthy
Self-responsible	Abdication of responsibility
Self-accountable	Lack of accountability
Assertiveness	Passivity or aggression

(Copyright Bill Longridge 1999)

Here are some further suggestions that I have put together over the years, from my own experience as well as working with clients on a 1to1 basis and in group workshops. They may give you food for thought as you put together your own list. Of course, some of the qualities outlined here may not be that important to you and you may have other qualities that are a higher priority to you. Go with what looks and feels right to you for your own list.

- Kind & thoughtful
- Loving - shows how he feels and about me & tells me regularly
- Caring & gentle
- Sensitive & intuitive
- Good morals and values
- Patient
- Has a big open heart
- Affectionate - sensual, passionate, a good kisser
- Physical spark between us, good sex life
- An even temperament
- Has healed from past hurts
- Emotionally intelligent - knows how he feels and why, can talk about feelings & be vulnerable
- Down to earth & humble
- Honest & reliable
- Trustworthy & trusting
- Good listener
- Can talk about things that he is worried about

- Fun to be with; light-hearted
- Very little or no ego
- Forgiving - does not hold a grudge
- Lovingly Assertive (not passive or aggressive)
- Generous - with time and money
- Committed to the relationship - (for the ups <u>and</u> the downs)
- Sexy
- Any specific physical characteristics that you are attracted to...
- Dresses nice, takes care of himself
- Healthy lifestyle - non-drinker, non-smoker
- Encourages me & is supportive of my work
- Optimistic outlook, into the law of attraction
- Grateful for all the blessings in his life
- Takes responsibility for whatever shows up in his life
- On his Spiritual path - prays, meditates, open to Angels & Spirit Guides, Healing etc.
- A Healer / Helps others in some way
- Open-minded and respectful of others
- Into self-development - reads books, does courses, attends workshops
- Self-aware
- Enjoys his work & is successful in his chosen career
- Intelligent
- Enjoys romantic dates & taking time out together
- Independent - we enjoy some time apart as well as togetherness
- Friendly and sociable
- Family-oriented
- Likes to cook (and we take turns cooking meals)
- We take turns helping with the kids and doing the chores/ things around the house
- Loves kids, would be / is a great father
- Gets on great with my child (children)
- Financially stable & is good with money
- Likes weekends away and holidays together...

This guy 'ordered' his ideal woman from the universe

I met with someone in 2014 (we will call him James) that I did some relationship coaching with about a year before. At that time, he had recently become single and was feeling sad, lonely and was beginning to give up hope of meeting that very special someone to share his life with (most of my clients are female, but I do get some men wanting to have relationship coaching as well). We spent those sessions getting really clear about what he wanted in his ideal partner (even down to her physical characteristics of dark colouring, long hair and small ears) and he wrote his list down in his weekly planner book that he used for work. At that time, the Angels showed me a vision of what she would look like and I shared this with him.

This "Designing your Ideal Partner" coaching exercise is very powerful and it can work very quickly. In fact, one of my female clients did this and then she met her new partner less than two weeks later! Two years later, they got married and are now in a very happy relationship.

I do have to point out that it does not always happen that quickly. Often, some time is needed to heal from your previous relationship and if that is the case, then I highly recommend taking the time to do that, so that you are not carrying that old emotional "baggage" into your next relationship (the exercises in this book will help you to work through any past hurt and pain, to process these and release them and be ready to love again with what I call an "open heart").

As James said "I have to admit I was sceptical. But I decided to give it a go. Initially I looked at my list every day, then over time less so. I just trusted that the universe would deliver. About a year later I met someone with all of the qualities that I was looking for. Once we became a couple, I even showed her the list – she could hardly believe it… and neither could I. She's amazing – everything I have always wanted in a partner. My list came true for me 100% and I just wanted to get in touch with you Ingrid to say "thank you." She even looks exactly as I had wrote on my list and has the cutest little ears I have ever seen, dark colouring due to her Spanish heritage and the most beautiful kind and loving heart."

Having seen them together now as a couple, I can confirm how happy they are as they plan their life together and she looks exactly as the Angels showed me in the vision I had the year before they met.

Exercise - designing your ideal partner

Take some time now and write down all of the qualities and attributes that you would like to attract in your new partner. Imagine that you could wave a magic wand and this person will appear as and when you are both ready, with all of these wonderful qualities that you so desire. For instance, what will he look like, what type of nature and personality will he have, what will it feel like to be in his presence, how will you spend your time together, what will he value and what will be important to him, how will he feel about you...?

Write down everything that comes to mind.

_____

_____

_____

_____

_____

_____

_____

_____

_____

_____

_____

_____

_____

_____

If you are already in a relationship and are deciding whether or not to continue with it, it can still be useful to review your list of attributes that your ideal partner would have - imagine that you are single and out there looking for a new partner. Write your list, as per the exercise above.

Then, go through your list and see how many of these attributes your current partner possesses - mark hard, by that I mean, is he **_consistently_** displaying these attributes that you are looking for - if he is, put a checkmark beside that one. If he is not, put an "X".

Then add up all your checkmarks and divide it by the total number of attributes on your list, then multiply by 100 to work out the percentage- e.g. if they had 12 of the 20 things that you are looking for, then they would have 60% of the attributes that you are looking for -

$$\frac{12}{20} \times 100 = 60\%$$

When I am coaching clients on their relationships and we review the score that they come up with, I tend to find the following -

Less than 60%	You are not very likely to be compatible with this person / have a happy relationship in the longer term. Over time, it is likely to feel like hard work and that something is missing
60 - 79%	You can look at the areas where your needs are not being met. If you are both willing to address these, then you could probably build on what you have to be more compatible, content and happy. If not, it would be best to separate

80% or above	You are very likely to have a compatible relationship with this person. Keep improving on what you have. Chances are, you will experience the blissful feelings associated with divine love - it will feel like heaven on earth.

I always encourage people to aim for a score of 80% or higher to be truly happy, content and compatible in their relationship.

Sometimes the clients that I work through this exercise with feel very sad that their relationship has a very low result of below 60% as they come to terms with the idea that they have grown apart from their partner over a period of time. However, they also realise that they deserve to be happy and so does their partner – it is a very kind act to end a relationship where there is low compatibility – you are letting go of someone that you have grown apart from and enabling the other person to connect with someone new that is compatible with them and on the same wavelength as them, with similar values and goals in life.

Priority List

Once you are clear about all of the wonderful characteristics and attributes that you want your ideal partner to have and have written these down in your ideal partner list, it is then time to prioritise them.

Prioritise these to your top 10 qualities (it may help to go through your list and give each one a score from 0-10 of how important each one is to you.

Then you can see which ones will be your top priority, start with your 10 scores, then your 9's and so on...):

_____
_____
_____
_____
_____
_____
_____
_____
_____
_____
_____
_____
_____
_____

At one stage, I narrowed my list down to the following 12 things:

My ideal partner list:

- Happy in himself and with his life
- Very spiritual (prays and meditates daily) & embodies the qualities of Divine Love
- Good balance of togetherness & independence
- Trustworthy and Trusting
- Has a big open heart, shows his feelings (is loving, sensual and romantic)
- Has very little ego - is humble and very self-aware
- Emotionally mature - deals with whatever comes up & takes responsibility (for everything that shows up in his life)
- Great chemistry - we adore each other
- A great Dad, great with my son
- Has an abundant attitude and practices the law of attraction
- Is a great communicator
- Fun, easy-going & self-secure

(I came up with 12 things for my list, so I trusted that and went with it. You may have just under ten or just over ten, as long as you are happy that it looks and feels right to you and is an accurate reflection of what you are looking for).

I then wrote these things, along with the date, on the back of one of my business cards and put this into my purse so that I would see it each day. I would then take a few moments each day to read over these qualities and it would help me to focus on what I was looking for in a potential partner.

I invite you to do the same - write your priority list of attributes onto a card or small piece of paper and carry it with you each day, taking at least 10 minutes in the morning and 10 minutes in the evening to visualize and feel what it would be like to have this person in your life.

> *"Yesterday I was clever, so I wanted to change the world.*
> *Today I am wise, so I am changing myself" - Rumi*

How do you measure up?

Now, go over your priority list - write it out again - and give *yourself* a score from 0-10 (with 10 being the highest) on how well you embody each of these qualities. Be honest!

Then commit to working on these areas until you can bring your own scores up towards a 10. Like attracts like and you will be much more likely to attract an amazing partner into your life if you have done the work on yourself to become the most amazing version of you that you can be.

Make a note of your scores for each quality here and then beside each quality write down your action plan of what you can do to be more patient, kind, or whatever the quality is that you wish to possess more of.

_____

_____

_____

_____

_____

_____

_____

_____

_____

_____

_____

_____

_____

_____

_____

_____

Ideal Behaviours

Another useful exercise to help you to become clearer about what you are looking for in your loving relationship with a partner, is to look at the behaviours that you did not like in previous relationships, then focus on the opposite (if you are currently with a partner, you can write down what you currently do not like and what you want instead).

I would like to share with you the things that I came up with when I did this exercise in my own life about one of my previous relationships, using the "-" sign for the negative trait or behaviour and the "+" sign for the opposite of each one (the positive trait or behaviour that I wanted to have more of in my life).

Exercise - Loving behaviours

- blaming me for his own shortcomings
+ taking full responsibility for everything that shows up in his life
- focusing on lack, poverty consciousness, negative beliefs about money
+ practicing the law of attraction, positive associations with money, prosperity consciousness
- low self-esteem / worthiness issues
+ good self-esteem, confident, good boundaries with other people, lovingly assertive
- looking to me for his main source of happiness and fulfilment
+ self-fulfilled and takes responsibility for his own happiness
- lack of trust (due to previous hurts from previous relationships)
+ complete trust in me
- sitting back, waiting for things to happen
+ proactively taking action everyday towards the things that he wants in life
- ignoring good advice and suggestions from others
+ being open to learning and advice from all sources (including me)
- not sharing things that were bothering him, (e.g. allowing pride to come up about finances, arguing and projecting rather than talking about what the issue was)
+ honest communication at all times (in kind and loving ways), even if this feels hard or uncomfortable
- past hurts from previous situations surfacing and affecting our relationship
+ has done very deep emotional healing on past hurts and issues so that they no longer have a strong emotional "charge"
- blaming me for things that he is not ready for or scared to do (projecting)

+ committed to his spiritual path & helping others
- making excuses for not doing the things he wants to do (self-sabotage)
+ living his spiritual practices every day (e.g. meditating, doing gratitude exercises, personal growth exercises)
- not contributing equally financially to the relationship, expecting me to pay more than my fair share of things
+ financially responsible and willing to help provide for our family
- fault finding, criticising
+ encouraging, supportive, being openly loving
- pursuing his own dreams whilst not supporting mine
+ supporting my hopes and dreams as well as his own

Take some time now to reflect on the things that you did not like in your previous relationships (or that you do not like in your current one) and list these here, along with the opposite behaviours that you would like to have more of in your life:

(You may want to cross out / put a line through the negative ones, as a sign that you no longer wish to have these in your life).

Now, make a new list with all the positive ones listed and read this aloud to yourself each day, put it up somewhere that you will see it regularly, imagine what it would be like and feel like to have a partner in your life that possessed all of these loving qualities.

My list of loving behaviours is as follows:

+ takes full responsibility for everything that shows up in his life
+ practices the law of attraction, positive associations with money, prosperity consciousness
+ good self-esteem, confident, good boundaries with other people, lovingly assertive
+ self-fulfilled and responsible for his own happiness
+ complete trust in me
+ proactively taking action everyday towards the things that he wants in life
+ being open to learning from all sources (including advice from me)
+ honest communication at all times (in kind and loving ways) in the present moment (keeping nothing back)
+ has done very deep emotional healing on past hurts and issues so that they no longer have an emotional "charge"
+ committed to his spiritual path & helping others
+ living his spiritual practices every day (e.g. meditating, doing gratitude exercises, personal growth exercises)
+ financially responsible and willing to help provide for our family
+ encouraging, supporting, being openly loving
+ supporting my hopes and dreams as well as his own

Take some time now to look over your list again and be completely honest with yourself about the ones that you need to do some work on - give yourself a score from 0-10 on how well you are currently displaying these behaviours, then commit to taking action to increase your own scores.

"Be the change you want to see in this world", Mahatma Gandhi

It is important to remember that in order to <u>attract in</u> all of these loving behaviours, you need to be **exhibiting** them in your own life. Like attracts like and you need to be living these qualities and behaving in these ways consistently in your own life to help you to enter into a state of readiness to then attract them to you.

Chapter 6

Using the law of attraction and other practical tips

Put very simply, the law of attraction is the name given to the belief that "like attracts like" and that by focusing on positive or negative thoughts, one can bring about positive or negative results.

Thoughts have an energy that attracts like energy. In her book and dvd called "The Secret" (2006), Rhonda Byrne tells us that in order to control this energy, you must practice three things:

- **Ask** - know what you want and ASK the universe / God for it
- **Believe** - have unwavering faith - know that the object of your desire is on its way
- **Receive** - be open to receiving it & know that you are worthy to receive it

This is known as **Deliberate Creation** - being able to <u>create your own reality</u>. This can be applied to your relationships, health, finances, career or any other aspect of your life. Everything is energy and by choosing to think positive thoughts, you will become a "Magnet", attracting positive situations, people and things to you.

Your thoughts become things. Trust your instincts - practice listening to your inner voice. It will guide you and magnetically move you towards receiving what you asked for.

If you then break what you want down into small steps, you can focus on one step at a time, which is very manageable, as opposed to becoming overwhelmed by thinking of the entire project or end result that may feel huge to you.

Esther and Jerry Hicks have written many wonderful books on this subject, including "The Law of Attraction - How to make it work for you" (Hay House, 2006).

In her book "The Soulmate Secret - Manifest the love of your life with the law of attraction", Arielle Ford has some wonderful tips and real life case studies on using the law of attraction to help to manifest the love of your life. She also shares her own life experiences of how she attracted her soulmate Brian Hilliard at age 44 using the principles of the law of attraction. It is an inspiring read with lots of practical tips and useful insights.

In her "Angel Therapy" Oracle Cards, Doreen Virtue shares the following wonderful exercise:

Write a letter to your twin flame's guardian angels. Begin the letter with "Dear Guardian Angels of my twin flame", and then express all of your feelings, thoughts and questions about your love life. End the letter by asking these angels to prepare you to meet your twin flame or soulmate and also to arrange this visit. You'll recognize your twin flame or soulmate immediately and there won't be any doubt in your heart or your mind when you're face-to-face with him or her.

Exercise - Positive visualisation of your loving partner

Find some quiet space where you will not be disturbed. Sit comfortably and make sure you are warm enough.

Close your eyes and focus on your abdominal breathing, taking some slow deep breaths in and out, allowing your mind and body to relax.

Once you feel relaxed, begin to visualise and feel your future exactly how you want it to be. Go ahead in time from now, see yourself achieving all of your goals and having a deep sense of satisfaction with your life.

What do you see in your mind's eye? Make the pictures bigger and brighter, as if you are watching a movie screen of your life in front of you.

How does it feel? Let these feelings intensify in your body and know that you have the power within you to achieve your dreams. Focus on some encouraging words – such as – "I know I can do this!", or "I will make this happen and I deserve this!"

Now, bring your attention to your love life in particular - imagine that you are with the partner of your dreams, who possesses all of the wonderful qualities that you desire (use your priority list and focus on your priority qualities that your partner will have...).

Notice what it feels like to be with this person, how it feels to be in their presence.

See yourselves spending time together, beginning to date and getting to know each other, building up a firm foundation of friendship, trust and mutual respect.

Notice what it is in particular that you love about him.

See yourselves a little bit further on, spending more time together, developing a deeper connection, spending time in each other's homes, how natural and easy it feels to be together.

Now, see yourself through his eyes, notice all of the qualities that he loves and adores about you, how it feels for him to be in your presence.

Notice all of the reasons why he has fallen in love with you.

When you are ready, you can bring your awareness back into the room you are in, have a little stretch and have a drink of water, if you wish.

Make a note of your insights here:

_____

_____

_____

_____

_____

_____

_____

_____

_____

_____

_____

_____

_____

_____

_____

_____

_____

_____

Do this often (ideally twice each day) and the subconscious part of your brain will accept these things as part of your reality and you will take action in your everyday life to support this vision and to make it happen for you.

I have done this visualisation exercise many times with clients and we have both been able to actually perceive things about their new partner, that they had not even met yet - for instance, their hair colour, personality, hobbies that they enjoy - they are always amazed when they meet that person and begin dating them. People often do not want this meditation to end, as they have truly tapped into the energy and the feeling of having this wonderful person in their life. As a result, they can feel a bit sad or deflated when they return to the present moment as there can be a feeling of longing to be with their new loving partner. It is this very longing at a soul level, however, that will spur them on and motivate them to do the work to prepare themselves to be ready for such a big love.

Connecting to your vision of divine love

We must believe in a particular intention before it can manifest in our lives. To assist with this, we can write it down then speak it aloud regularly (twice a day, once in the morning and once in the evening) and then take action to support the manifestation.

Make a conscious commitment today to manifest divine love in your life. Write it down, write it in you journal, put it on your vision board and tell others about it. Write your personal power statement – a clear and concise statement of your intention to manifest divine love.

For instance:

I am committed to having an amazingly deep, intimate and loving connection with the love of my life, my twin flame, sharing in a divine purpose and in divine love. I am ready for a happy and

committed relationship and I am willing to do whatever it takes to enable this to manifest in my life.

Exercise – write your power statement and state your intention

---

Share your power statement and intention with at least one other like-minded person, who can help hold a space for you to manifest this in your life. Then take one inspired action towards it.

> *"Take the first step in faith. You don't have to see the whole staircase. Just take the first step". Martin Luther King Jr.*

Vision of divine love

One of the most powerful tools of manifestation that I have come across is to write your vision statement. Really go into what it will look like and feel like to have divine love in your life and write it all down on paper. Here is mine that I wrote. I would read this aloud every morning and every evening and really felt what it would feel like to share my life with this wonderful person.

<u>**My vision of divine love**</u>

I have connected with my divine loving partner/Twin Flame. I feel so content, peaceful and at ease.

We both do work that we love and feel so fulfilled, sharing our gifts with others and helping and supporting people through difficult times. We do work that excites us and delegate to others the other tasks that need done, so our time is devoted to fulfilling our highest potential.

We have created a warm, cosy, beautiful family home together, filled with love. It reflects who we are as well as who our children are.

Family is a key priority for us and we love our time together and fun days out. We consciously balance our time between work, rest and play (for our family, ourselves and as a couple).

We regularly take time together as a couple, having dates and feeling the excitement and the anticipation of being together ("butterflies").

We have such beautiful emotional intimacy – we can share and talk about anything. He is my best friend, my confidante, the first person I share my deepest truths with, my hopes and dreams, my hearts deepest desires and also my fears and worries.

There are healthy boundaries in the relationship, whereby we are both lovingly assertive and aware of our needs and how to express and communicate these in kind and loving ways.

There is a very high level of self-awareness – we each notice our feelings as and when they arise, can express and process these as a matter of priority, releasing and healing them. We support each other in this and hold a loving space for each other, as and when required.

There is a healthy balance of togetherness and independence. We each encourage the others hopes and dreams and support each other's development and growth.

We make a great team, with both of us helping out, willingly doing extra at times to support each other (if the other is busy or stressed).

We share a beautifully sensual, affectionate and passionate connection. We show our feelings for each other with frequent touching, holding and kissing. We regularly take time together to enjoy being intimate together (both physically and emotionally). We experience a very deep connection, beyond merely physical. There is a knowingness at a soul level.

We are conscious parents and we encourage our children to be who they are, to express themselves, to explore their gifts and talents and they know that they are fully supported and that they are loved unconditionally.

There is a strong sense of integrity in all that we do and we live our values. We enjoy spending our time with spiritual, loving people that we admire and can learn from.

We have processed and cleared all of our past hurts so that we can love each other with big open hearts. We deal with any issues or fears immediately, so that we can radiate a high vibration of energy, dealing with anything that comes up in a timely way and consciously taking steps to raise our energy, as and when required.

There is complete trust and respect for each other. I trust him with my heart completely. There is a feeling of knowing that this is right, that it is meant to be.

We each have our own routine and space to work. There is a sense of freedom and space, with each taking responsibility for our own lives and work.

We experience financial abundance and ease. Bills are paid on time and savings are put by. We experience a wonderful sense of security and we feel relaxed and calm about this area of our life. We regularly have rewards and treats (such as weekends away, holidays, etc.)

There is complete emotional honesty and if any egoic thoughts do come up, we discuss these and share what we are feeling with open hearts, acceptance, non-judgement and loving kindness. We are real and authentic with each other, as well as holding a safe space to be vulnerable at times.

We are each other's greatest supporters – we inspire and cheer each other on with ideas, suggestions, encouragement and support.

There is a gentleness and tenderness that underpins all that we do. Harmony, ease and grace are key priorities for us and we deal with anything that may threaten these in a timely and loving way.

We each stand fully in the power of who we are. There is a lack of dependence on each other, of not "needing" the other, of feeling resilient and knowing that we are each "enough" as we are. We then enhance each other's lives from this place of inner strength and power. We are both at ease with who we are and we each radiate the divine essence of who we are into the world.

Exercise - write your vision statement. Really go into what it will look like and feel like to have divine love in your life.

_____

_____

_____

_____

_____

_____

_____

_____

_____

_____

_____

_____

_____

_____

_____

_____

_____

_____

_____

(continue on a separate page if necessary)

"Consciousness precedes all matter" – Einstein

Vision board

You can also make a **Vision Board (or Dream Board)** of your ideal life - use a canvas or notice board and put on inspiring words and pictures to reflect all of the things that you wish to have in your life, whether it is your dream home, good health, vitality, a new car, holidays you want to go on, a new job, starting your own business, writing a book, a loving relationship with your dream partner - whatever it is that you want. Once it is completed, keep it somewhere where you will see it each day, to help motivate and inspire you towards your goals.

You can then also make a **Vision Board** dedicated <u>entirely</u> to your new partner. Put on photos that resonate with you about this person, places you want to visit together, words that describe him and how it feels to have this person in your life, photos of couples being affectionate together, going for walks - whatever it is that you wish to do together. Keep this somewhere where you will see it each day so that you can remind yourself on a regular basis of all the qualities that you are focused on attracting in your ideal partner.

See it and feel it everyday

Spend at least ten minutes, twice a day, once in the morning and once in the evening, visualising and feeling your wonderful new partner in your life. Allow yourself this time to daydream. Read aloud your Vision of Divine Love and really allow yourself to feel the contentment, happiness, joy, bliss and even excitement that will surround you when you do meet this person.

As you do your visualisation each day and read your vision statement aloud, notice what it *<u>feels like</u>* to be in this person's presence. It is interesting to note that your ideal partner may not look exactly how you <u>think</u> they will look - they may look a little bit different to the type of person that you are usually attracted to, but it is your ***<u>energetic</u>*** ***<u>connection</u>*** to this person that is the key element to your relationship and your spiritual/divine connection to each other.

> *"Beauty is not in the face. Beauty is a light in the heart"* Khalil Gibran

<u>*Exercise – Connecting to people's energy*</u>

As you go about your normal day to day routine, notice what it <u>feels</u> like to be in other people's presence. What qualities do you like or admire in these people?

Do you feel energised or drained after spending time with them? Practice noticing and feeling other people's energy regularly.

Make a note of your insights here:

_____

_____

_____

_____

_____

_____

_____

_____

_____

_____

_____

_____

_____

_____

_____

_____

_____

_____

_____

_____

_____

Prepare your living environment

If you have been single for a while, chances are your living space may not be a true reflection of your desire to attract in your new partner. Does it have a balance of male and female within it? For instance, would someone of the opposite sex feel comfortable spending time there and eventually sleeping over? Is there excessive pink and feminine decor? What could you do to make it more welcoming to your new partner?

Perhaps freshening up with some new paint on the walls, bringing new colour to a room by getting a new rug or throw cushions, having some mugs that would be more suited to a male guest, buying a new set of towels and spare toothbrush for when he does spend the night, or even making some room in a wardrobe or drawer for when he will spend more time there regularly.

I personally did all of these things, plus I purchased a new bedside lamp, so that we could each have our own light by the bed to read at night, as I love to read and learn about new things.

One of my clients, we will call her June, faithfully wrote out her list of qualities, made her beautiful vision board to reflect these (she included romantic pictures from magazines, poems that she loved, words that described her dream man, as well as some sensual and passionate pictures). She then had the wonderful idea of cleaning her ensuite bathroom beside her bedroom to prepare it for her new partner to come into her life. She bleached the tiles and scrubbed them with a toothbrush, bought a new set of towels in a colour that a man would like, then also purchased some male toiletries and a toothbrush that her new partner can use when he eventually stays overnight at her home. What a wonderful welcome for her new partner!

Prepare yourself

As well as doing the inner work on yourself with the exercises in this book, it can be useful to also give yourself a make-over on the outside. A friend of mine, Anne Rowney, is a Fashion Stylist and I was lucky enough to win a wardrobe review and make-over with her (a raffle prize at one of her events). She very gently went through all of my clothes and we reviewed what did not suit me, what no longer fit (and was not likely to ever fit me again!), as well as how to co-ordinate outfits together and colours that suit me, as well as some suggestions of things to buy to fill in the gaps in my wardrobe, at prices that I could afford (I was a single Mum at the time and was not earning a lot of money). We cleared out three big bags to donate to the charity shop, three to go up to the attic, and two to be recycled. She even went through my underwear and pyjama drawer. We got rid of some old things to make way for some new ones, which I could then wear when I did get together with my new man for dates and days out together.

This really helped to boost my confidence, as I then looked and felt good, in clothes that suited me and flattered my shape and colouring. I felt more at ease at work, on my time off and also when I began dating again. It was also easier to put outfits together, once my wardrobe had been organised and the old things cleared out of it.

Developing an attitude of gratitude

We can use gratitude as a daily practice, to put our attention on all of the things that we are blessed with in our lives. We can choose to develop an "Attitude of Gratitude". This means being grateful for all of the blessings that you have each day and writing down your gratitude list or mentally giving thanks for your blessings each day. Even if you are going through a difficult or challenging time, chances are that you can still count 10 blessings with ease (for instance, having a warm bed to sleep in, a roof over your head, enough food to eat, the love of a family member or friend in your life, etc...).

Do your gratitude list every day for the next 21 days - and then it will become a habit for you to do regularly. Observe how this affects your life - as you begin to "attract" more positive things into your life, as gratitude is a very powerful emotion and can help to "attract" other positive things into your life.

Exercise - Take some time every morning and every evening to reflect on 10 things that you feel grateful for and write these into your journal over the next 21 days (and beyond).

"Deep at the center of my being there is an infinite well of gratitude.
I now allow this gratitude to fill my heart, my body, my mind, my consciousness,
my very being. This gratitude radiates out from me in all directions, touching

everything in my world, and returns to me as more to be grateful for.
The more gratitude I feel, the more I am aware that
the supply is endless." Louise L Hay

Exercise - Letter of gratitude for your new partner - write a letter of gratitude for your new partner. Focus on all of the qualities that they will possess and write it in the present tense, as if they are already in your life. Really immerse yourself in this and let yourself feel what it would feel like to have this person in your life. Then read this aloud twice a day as you feel these wonderful feelings in your body.

If you wish to take it a step further, you can also write a letter of gratitude to yourself from your new partner, focusing on all of the qualities that you possess that they love, so you are seeing yourself through their eyes. You can then also read this aloud twice a day, allowing yourself to feel and connect with their love for you.

Here is my letter of gratitude for my new partner (that I wrote at a time when I was single) –

Dear Angels,

Thank you for my wonderful partner who gets on well with my son Lewis and would like another child together. He is a great role model and father-figure. I love seeing how much he enjoys being a Dad and the joy on his face in all the little things that we share with our children - from the moment that they are born, to their every little achievement as they learn and grow - every day we get to spend with them is a blessing to us and a gift directly from God. Ours is a true partnership - both helping out and taking turns with whatever needs to be done.

Thank you for helping us to heal from all our past hurts and to be able to love each other and our children with big, open hearts and for us to feel safe with being intimate and vulnerable together - to talk about our hopes, dreams and also our fears. We show our feelings towards each other, are affectionate and tell each other regularly how we feel. We both feel truly loved, adored and cherished.

I love that we are both committed to our relationship and our family and are 100% there for each other - for the ups and the downs of life. We handle things as a team, whatever comes our way. I love his optimistic outlook on life and we have great fun "creating" the life that we want together - for us and our family. We take comfort from knowing that the challenges in our lives are merely lessons that we need to learn to evolve and grow into who we need to be.

He is sexy and there is a real physical spark between us. I find him so attractive and love just being in his presence and being close to him and feeling his beautiful energy - it is like standing next to an Angel. He is very humble and down-to-earth and friendly and sociable - he could talk to and relate to anyone from all walks of life.

He is so supportive of me and my hopes and dreams and I feel so inspired by him and all his encouragement to go after my dreams and make them come true.

I love the fact that he has very little / no ego and that he is on his Spiritual path and helps others. Thank you for the wonderful things that we learn together - the books that we read, the courses we attend and workshops that we go to. We are always open to learning new things, to be closer to God and the Angels and to become more enlightened and true images of God and the Angels here on earth.

Love from Ingrid xx

Letter to Me – I also wrote this letter to myself, from my "new partner"

Dear Ingrid,

Thank you for coming into my life - every day I thank God that I share my life with such a caring, loving and kind person. There is a light that radiates from you - you are pure LOVE and you share this with everyone that you come into contact with.

I love how you help and inspire other people - you support them through their greatest challenges and darkest hours, giving them hope and helping them to find their true path through life towards enlightenment and to be closer to God and the Angels. I love your strength - you are one of the strongest people I know, but also the most nurturing and gentle.

You are so beautiful and attractive to me - I could look at you all day and I love holding you in my arms, being near you, like we are two halves of the same whole.

Thank you for the joy that you bring to me every day - the little things that you do for me, listening when I am down or worried, encouraging me and inspiring me to be the best person, partner and father that I can be.

Thank you for the warm, cosy, welcoming home that we have created together - I feel so at ease here and there is nowhere else I would rather be.

Thank you for appreciating all that I am and all that I do for you, our family and others. It makes me want to do even more.

You are such a wonderful Mother - it is as if you were born to be a Mummy - our children just adore you and really appreciate all that you do for them. You are so patient with them and I love that you simply allow them to be who they are and support them to be the best version of themselves that they can be. We have so much fun together on our family days out, trips to the beach, the forest and fun nights in together.

You are everything that I asked for in a partner and more - we really make a great team and I feel so strong when I have you by my side, with your unfaltering love and support.

Thank you for your patience and for being so committed to me, to us and to our family. It gives me such a strong foundation - where I know that I can do anything that I set my mind to and create an amazing and wonderful life!

From your beloved husband

xx

"Be grateful for what you have. You will end up having more" Oprah Winfrey

Chapter 7

What is holding you back?

"Your task is not to seek for love, but merely to seek and find all the barriers within yourself that you have built against it." Rumi

What is holding you back from experiencing divine love fully in your life?

There can be many things that can get in the way and hold us back from divine love. Some of the ones that come up when I am working with clients include:

1) Outdated negative beliefs (e.g. there are no good men out there etc.)
2) Hurts from previous relationships that have not been processed and healed (or even from childhood)
3) Repeating an unhealthy pattern of who we are attracted to (rather than being conscious of the learning and how we need to change and grow beyond that)
4) Fear of getting hurt (again)
5) Low self-worth (e.g. who would want me? I am too old, not successful enough, too overweight... too anything)

6) Worry about what other people would think (e.g. my family would not approve, none of my friends have happy relationships, etc.)

7) Has not fully healed from and integrated the learning from a previous relationship (e.g. still in love with an ex, or grieving the loss of their partner who has passed away etc.)

8) Procrastination (e.g. I will start dating next year; when the kids leave home; when I get promoted; when I retire... etc.)

9) Fear that they will 'lose' something, such as their freedom or identity if they get together with someone new (due to this happening with a previous partner)

10) Does not believe that someone so wonderful actually exists

I wonder if any of these apply to you? Or perhaps something else? The good news is that these are just thoughts and thoughts can be processed, healed, transformed and released.

Exercise - what is in the way for you?

- *What might be in the way of you attracting in your dream partner?*
- *Are you afraid of trusting again, afraid of getting hurt if it does not work out?*
- *Do you feel that you are a worthy partner for this person?*
- *Do you believe that someone this amazing actually exists out there in the world?*
- *Or perhaps there is something else in the way for you...?*

Whatever your fears or blocks, rest assured that once you are aware of what they are, you can do some work on them.

Make a note of them here-

_____

_____

_____

_____
_____
_____
_____
_____
_____
_____
_____
_____
_____
_____
_____
_____
_____
_____
_____
_____
_____
_____
_____
_____

I often use a combination of Life Coaching, Energy work and EFT tapping with people (and of course, in my own life) to look at what is in the way for them and then we work on it together. I have witnessed wonderful results where past hurts have been transformed, the most difficult divorce, break up or trauma healed, negative beliefs dissolved and healthy ones instilled, fears eliminated and hopefulness embraced once more.

Using EFT Tapping on fears or blocks

-10 -9 -8 -7 -6 -5 -4 -3 -2 -1 0 +1 +2 +3 +4 +5 +6 +7 +8 +9 +10
Negative Emotions　　　　　　　*Neutral*　　　　　　*Positive Emotions*

(adapted from www.1-EFT.com)

Case Study - using EFT to help to heal a relationship break up

I was coaching Iris (that we heard about in Chapter 4) about preparing to date again, following a difficult break up.

Her score on the SUE scale was -9 when we discussed how she was feeling about possibly meeting someone and going on a first date. She felt very fearful and uncomfortable about this, as she was associating the upset, arguing and aggression that occurred at the end of her previous relationship with having a new man in her life. In other words, she was thinking:

A New Man = arguing, pain, aggression

However, this was not based on logic or evidence of this new man, it was being based on what had happened with her previous partner at the end of their relationship, just before the break up.

We made a note of her score and began tapping, doing a full round (as outlined in Chapter 2) - starting with both hands over the heart chakra, saying aloud, **"this fear"**.

We continued to say these words aloud, while tapping on the following points, (remembering to tap lightly) -

- The top of the head
- The third eye (in the middle of the forehead)
- Eyebrow - at the inner beginning point of your eyebrow
- The outer corner of the eye
- Under the eye (directly under the pupil if you are looking straight ahead)
- Under the nose (in the middle of the fleshy part between your nose and upper lip)
- Under the mouth (in the middle of the indentation of your chin)
- Under the collarbone

- On the thumb, at the side of the nail bed
- Then at the side of the nail of each of your four fingers - index, middle, ring and little finger
- Finally, on the Karate Chop point, halfway down the side of your hand (below your little finger)

Then we finished by putting both hands flat on the centre of the chest (the heart chakra) and taking three deep breaths in and out (not saying anything this time, just allowing the energy to settle). She then had a sip of water (which can be helpful when doing energy work of any kind).

After this one round of tapping, her score moved up the SUE scale slightly, to -6.

When we checked in with how Iris was feeling, she shared that in one of their arguments, her ex-partner had become very angry and aggressive and unreasonable and she had to threaten to call the police if he did not calm down. I could see how upset she was as she shared this with me, as she said, **"he was horrible, and I was scared"**.

So we did a full round of tapping again, using these words, **"he was horrible, and I was scared"**.

She released alot of the energy associated with this event that occurred and felt stronger in herself at the end of this round of tapping. Her score now was up to 0, where she felt neutral about this event, as she said, **"I am glad that it is over"**.

We then did a full round of tapping on this wording, **"I am glad that it is over"**. Her score then increased to a +4.

She confirmed that she was grateful for the learning from that relationship, but that they had grown apart. We discussed what Iris had to offer to a new partner, all of her special and unique qualities, as well as reviewing her ideal partner list that she had already written prior to our session. We then moved into tapping on the positive aspects of the situation.

We did a full round of tapping using the words **"I am committed to my vision of divine love."** Her score increased to +7.

Then another round using the words **"I am ready for my happy ending"** and Iris' score this time came right up to a +10.

During the EFT tapping session, Iris let go of the fear and negative associations that were still lingering from the end of her previous relationship. She also let go of the hope of having a happy ending with her ex-partner, who she had grown apart from, but she still held her vision of divine love and reconnected to the idea of her happy ending with a new partner.

When I checked in with her a few days later, she no longer felt fearful and anxious about the possibility of a first date with a new partner. Instead, she was feeling the normal flutters in her tummy, also known as "butterflies", at the thought of meeting a wonderful new man, while at the same time treating herself to a new hair style and some new clothes that she could wear while beginning to date again.

Exercise - what is in the way for you?

Go back over your list of what is in the way for you, then taking each one in turn, do some tapping on it, as per the example outlined above. Check in on the SUE scale to check your score and how you are feeling about this issue, then use whatever words come to mind as you do a full round of EFT Tapping.

Make a note of your progress and your scores here.

Keep going with further rounds of EFT tapping, checking your scores after each round and using the words that come to you and that feels right to you.

Have a look also at the EFT Tapping videos on my website www. ingriddarragh.com and on my Facebook page "Ingrid Darragh – Divine Love", showing examples and client case studies of how to use Tapping to deal with fears and blocks, to become unstuck and to feel ready to move forward again.

Once your fears and blocks are processed and healed, you will be another step closer to manifesting the love of your life into your life. If you feel stuck, work with a Life Coach, join one of my upcoming Teleclasses, sign up for some 1to1 coaching with me, or book in for one of my Workshops to get the extra support that you may need.

Angel Jess

I have to be honest and admit that I did everything that I have outlined within this book, every exercise, every visualisation, and every technique and yet, I still felt stuck - that divine love was on its way to me but never quite arrived. As a Life Coach and Emotional Healer, I knew that I had to take responsibility for this and to be prepared to look deep within myself as to why and then commit to dealing with whatever I found there.

What I came up with was very interesting:

1) There was a part of me that did not believe that this amazing guy actually existed. It seemed "too good to be true".
2) There was another part of me that found it hard to believe that this amazing guy would want to be with ME. That I would be everything that he was looking for.

I did some work on this first 1) negative belief that was holding me back using EFT tapping (and another Energy Psychology technique called Tapas Acupressure Technique (TAT). I got my final score right up to a +10 and finished with the wording "My 'Mr too good to be true' is now 'My Reality'".

I then examined the reason for this second 2) belief and found that I felt somehow inadequate or not "good enough" because of the things that had happened to me in my life. Following the pituitary illness that I had, plus the two extreme cases of PTSD (Post Traumatic Stress Disorder), I sometimes would feel very tired, particularly during periods of high levels of stress or too many consecutive busy days in a row. My body did not seem to process the stress chemicals such as adrenaline and cortisol as well as it did prior to these events.

I have therefore learned to pace myself, rest when I need to and manage situations that are stressful or highly charged with adrenaline and find that I am now probably about 90-95% back to what my abilities were in this area of my life, but yet this fear remained. Then the universe sent me a lesson that demonstrated the learning to me so much more directly and deeply than anything else could have.

In 2011 I came across a picture and description online through a friend, of a little stray dog that was at the local pound and that needed a new loving home, a cross between a Bichon Frise and a Poodle. The description said that she had one leg missing and had some health issues so she would need immediate attention from a Vet. The following day, I felt a compelling urge to drive to the pound to see her. As someone who follows my intuitive feelings on a regular basis, I trusted this urge and went to the pound right away. She did indeed require urgent attention. As well as her missing limb, she was passing blood and her fur was very matted from living on the streets for such a long period of time - you could actually see the fleas jumping off her skin. For a moment, I considered walking away and making my excuses as to why I could not take her with me. But then I checked in with my intuition - in front of me on my left side I put the option of not taking her with me, on my right, the option of taking her and providing a home for her. All of my energy and attention went to second option, so I made the necessary arrangements and filled in the paperwork, even though I had never had a dog before and knew there would be a hefty Vets bill running into several hundreds of pounds that I knew I did not have readily available, so I would need to find the extra money. Somehow, I knew that everything was as it should be and that everything that we needed was being taken care of. I trusted this feeling.

So I took the bit of rope that was all they had to act as a lead for her and I walked her out through the car park. As I watched her walk in her own little way that she had adapted to take account of her health issues, I could not help but notice how happy she was to be alive and her gratitude was overwhelming. I realised then that I had fallen in love with her, with her spirit, with who she was at the core of her being. I also realised that her spirit was developed as a direct result of all of her challenges, all of her life experiences - it was so beautiful for me to be in the presence of her spirit that it was actually breath-taking.

At that moment, I realised that my new partner would love me for who I am, would love my spirit, the essence of which has been altered and adapted with each of the experiences and challenges that I have faced in my life. I also connected with a deeper level of love for myself, as well as a deep respect and admiration for all that I had experienced and overcome in my life.

I also knew that if I felt tired sometimes and wanted to take some time to pace myself or recharge, that it would be of absolutely no concern to him, that it would be something that he would lovingly support as and when it may show up.

After discussion with my son Lewis, we called her Angel Jess, known simply as Jess. The eventual Vets bills did run into many hundreds of pounds to treat her tumour that she had and the surgery that was necessary. The joy that I was to witness in her was such a gift to me - she was so grateful to be alive and to have a warm and loving home to live in. I was guided to take her to a particular Vet, who was so wonderful in his treatment and helping Jess with her health issues, as well as being very patient and allowing me to pay what I could afford in a few instalments over a period of time (as I did not have any insurance for her at that time).

Indeed, once I did the work on these two old beliefs, I began dating someone a month later (yes, it can work that quickly!) that I had known as a friend. As we continued to date and build on our friendship that we already had, we became closer and prepared to share with the other about our developing feelings for each other. The words that he chose to express his feelings towards me are pertinent and deserving of mention here, as he said to me "I love your spirit", rather than the usual "I love you" that people tend to share with each other. The relationship ended, for various reasons, but the learning and insights that I obtained about love were very precious ones that will always stay with me.

We only had little Jess in our lives for three short months, but I will always be grateful to her for coming into our family and supporting me to learn the true lesson of my self-worth, to know that I deserve to share my life with an equally amazing spiritual partner, that we would love each other at such a deep and spiritual level and that what I had mistakenly perceived to be "flaws" were actually the very experiences that supported my soul to grow into the evolved spirit that I have now become. Thank you, Angel Jess.

This deeper level of self-love was actually a key step, a foundation that was necessary for what was to come - a deep level of unconditional love, mutual appreciation and acceptance of each other, complete trust, emotional responsibility, deep contentment and compatibility, open-hearted and authentic connection, an equal balance of giving and receiving and commitment to being of service here on earth, with humility and grace.

> *"At the highest level, life is a process of spiritual evolution… We are here to dissolve our barriers to love." Miranda Macpherson*

Chapter 8

The importance of forgiveness

"People are often unreasonable and self-centered. Forgive them anyway.
If you are kind, people may accuse you of ulterior motives. Be kind anyway.
If you are honest, people may cheat you. Be honest anyway.
If you find happiness, people may be jealous. Be happy anyway.
The good you do today may be forgotten tomorrow. Do good anyway.
Give the world the best you have and it may never be enough.
Give your best anyway.
For you see, in the end, it is between you and God.
It was never between you and them anyway."
Mother Teresa

To forgive is to – *"stop resenting someone for something they have done", Collins English Dictionary.*

In all likelihood, we all have someone or even many people that we need to forgive - someone from our past that has hurt us, something that happened during our childhood, someone that wronged us at school or during our working lives, or the one that comes up probably most often – someone that has hurt us in a romantic relationship. The person that we need to forgive may not even be on this planet anymore. Chances are, we each have to also forgive ourselves for something.

The teachings of A Course in Miracles, published by the Foundation for Inner Peace, tells us that unforgiveness is at the root of all illness and disharmony in the body. Indeed, by choosing to harbour strong or even extreme feelings of unforgiveness, these feelings are held in the body and can be expressed as very strong emotions - such as anger, sadness, resentment - even rage.

It has been said that not forgiving someone is like continually sipping from a cup of poison – and hoping that it will kill the other person, whereas in truth, it only harms us. So whenever someone has hurt us and we delay forgiveness, we extend the period of our hurt and therein choose to hold onto the pain that we experienced.

Now, I am not saying that forgiveness means that you have to become the person's "best friend" that wronged you, but it does mean releasing the toxic feelings that you may have been holding inside in relation to that person. It is also important to note here that forgiving another person does not mean that we are condoning what they did (their actions) or what they stand for in this world, i.e. we can condemn the behavior or actions of that person, but still choose to forgive them.

It is actually an act of "self-love" to acknowledge that you deserve a happy, healthy and prosperous life, free from the pain and burden of unforgiveness. When we choose to forgive and recognise that we are willing to forgive, this is the first step in the forgiveness process. With this willingness comes the beginning of the healing process, which can be on a physical, mental, emotional and spiritual level.

You have heard people say, "I forgive, but I won't forget" and that is okay. Forgetting might take some time, depending on the amount of hurt that you experienced and in some instances, forgetting may never happen. By remembering, it may serve to protect you from something similar happening to you again in the future, much as a child who burns his hand on the hot stove learns to be more careful the next time that he is standing in front of that same stove, or something of a similar threat to his well-being.

So you might be reading this and be thinking, that is all well and good, and I do want to forgive, but I feel stuck and just don't seem to be able to get through it. We therefore need to examine what might get in the way of us being ready to forgive, for instance:

1) **"I am not letting him off the hook that easy"** - the hurt that you experienced might be so severe, so strong, so traumatic even, that you are struggling to bring yourself to forgive this person. Or that person may experience no regrets or remorse or may not even be aware of the fact that they caused you so much hurt or pain, so it would feel illogical to you to even consider forgiving them for what they did

2) **The anger (or even rage) that you feel has you frozen, unable to move forward** - you may not be able to see past this anger and feel that it overwhelms you to the point where it is affecting your day to day life, your relationships with others, your work etc. and you do not know what to do about it

3) **You are stuck as you do not know how to deal with your anger** - for you to be able to move forward, it may be necessary for you to process your anger (which we will look at soon as part of this Forgiveness Process). However, if you are a very kind and gentle person, you may not be used to expressing your anger or dealing with conflicts. This may be keeping you stuck.

4) **Fear of it happening again** - you may have a fear that if you forgive this person, they or someone else might hurt you again to the same degree that you experienced this time round.

Or maybe there is some other reason that you are stuck? Whatever the reason, unforgiveness can cost us both health and energy and it has been said that it can even contribute to stress in our bodies, illnesses and even lead to anxiety, depression and dis-ease.

In order to help us to be ready to forgive, it is important to safely and privately release the anger that we are holding inside about the other person or situation. The safe release of anger honors the part of us that has felt violated and hurt. Anger can be safely and privately released without the need to actually communicate with the other person - we do not need to speak to them or post a letter to them for us to receive the healing. This release of anger can then help to clear the way for forgiveness.

We need to dispel the illusion that forgiveness somehow diminishes us, or lets the other person "win". Remember why you are doing this – as an act of loving yourself and to free yourself from the burden of holding onto old hurts and pains associated with unforgiveness.

So what happens when the logical part of us (the head) wants to forgive the person or situation that has hurt us so much, but we cannot progress any further? We feel stuck. The emotional part of us (the heart) hears our pleas for forgiveness, it may even want to go ahead and forgive - but when it comes right down to it, this part of us can refuse to budge - because it was so deeply wounded by what happened. That is how I felt when I went through my marital separation and divorce- I wanted to forgive, but I felt stuck. The anger, rage and resentment that I felt within me were beginning to change who I was. This did not sit well with me, because I knew who I truly was. I remembered my kind, gentle, caring nature that was there before these things happened to me and I wanted to get these qualities - who I truly am - back. I was focused on wanting to serve others as a Spiritual Life Coach and Healer and I also wanted to become a Mother at some stage in the future and it was these very qualities that I knew I wanted to possess, especially in these two areas of my life. So I continued on the next stage of my Healing Quest and set out to learn more about how I could forgive and move forward with my life again, free from the anger and resentment that would overwhelm me at times.

At that time, I attended the annual N. Ireland Natural Health Fair - in November 2006. This is an annual fair in Belfast with workshops, talks and demonstrations of various therapies. I attended a talk given by Bill Longridge - a Spiritual Psychotherapist and Life Coach whose business was called "Happiness Matters" - and one of his main subject areas for his talk was on Forgiveness. I truly believe that God and the Angels brought Bill into my life at that time, to support me with what I needed to learn about forgiveness. I introduced myself at the end of his talk and then rang him a few weeks later to arrange an appointment with him. I had a few sessions with Bill and was quickly in touch with my Anger and learning about new things that would help me to forgive. Bill and I became great friends and after I finished my sessions with him, we met up regularly to share books and personal development DVDs and to "coach" and encourage each other on our Life's Paths. He would call me a "Superstar" and tell me that I was going to set the world alight. Even when I was very ill, he would tell me "You cannot deprive the world of your gifts, Ingrid" and would encourage me to focus on writing and starting to coach others.

Bill passed away in December 2008 after a very progressive illness. Even in the days before his passing, we discussed the learning that we had both gained from having a very challenging period of illness in our lives. We were both very focused on seeing the learning from the things that came up in our lives and how it could enlighten us on our Spiritual Path. I was so impressed with the way that he chose to continue to focus on gratitude and to count his blessings each day and also to continue to support others right up to his last days on this earth.

I am very blessed that Bill came into my life, he was a great spiritual teacher and an enlightened soul and I learned many great things from him, as did many others.

After Bill's passing, I met his former wife, Sonia Longridge. Sonia was the founder of the Natural Health Fair and has since established the Natural Therapies Directory NI, an online directory. Sonia and I became great friends and we meet up regularly to support and encourage each other in our various endeavours, one of which being the writing of this book. Bill also continues to guide and encourage me from the spirit world - I sometimes receive messages from him when I am meditating and he continues to offer his wonderful insightful guidance and loving advice as I progress along my Path. Thank you, Bill.

Forgiveness Process

*Please note that if you have been through a very traumatic experience,
take the time to discuss this with an appropriate Therapist before
proceeding with the Forgiveness Process. Trust your instincts relating to
this and enlist the help of a good Therapist, should you need it, to keep
yourself safe and to avoid the possibility of re-traumatising yourself by
bringing up these memories again without the necessary support.*

What I am going to share with you now is the Forgiveness Process that
I have developed as a result of my experiences and my search to heal
myself. I can assure you that it does work - it has for me and for many
of my clients. You do need to do each step fully, especially the Hurts
List and the Anger releasing. You may even have to go back over these
two steps a few times before you feel ready to forgive. It is important
to note that forgiveness work can be draining to start with, but then
frees up energy later on – you may need to allow some time for this,
particularly if you have very deep hurts to heal, or hurts that come
from many different people or situations. Do them one at a time and
see what pace works best for you.

Make a conscious decision to be there for yourself and nurture yourself
through this forgiveness process, however long it takes to complete.
Enlist the help of supportive people from as many sources as you
can – such as: good friends, family, a coach, therapist, the Angels
or any Spirit Guides that you work with, complementary therapists,
etc. - as you feel appropriate to support you. Also notice if you feel
drained by other people's energy while you are working through this
process - be very gentle with yourself at this time and choose to spend
time with gentle, loving, caring people, who can support you on your
Healing journey.

My Mentor Coach and friend, Bill Longridge, used to say that it is by
going "into the wilderness" that we find our true selves. I went into the
"wilderness" to do my forgiveness work, but I had my home comforts

of a fridge full of nurturing food, hot baths in the evening and lots of rest and sleep to support me through this process.

Make a list of some nurturing things that you could do for yourself, should you need them at any stage of this process:

1) How can you nurture yourself through this Forgiveness Process?

For instance, having a warm bath, cooking a nice meal, listening to relaxing music, having an early night, going for a walk, reading some inspiring books or watching uplifting DVDs, being pampered- for instance having a massage, getting your hair done, spending time with positive, uplifting people….etc.

2) Whom, or what, from the past do you need to forgive? (If there is more than one, please work through this process one at a time for each).

---

3) Hurts List

Now, make a list of the hurts that came up for you – from this person or situation. Write down as many as you can and be as thorough as possible.

---

4) Release each Hurt and the associated emotions

It is important to note that releasing anger can be very draining so it is a good idea to limit a session of anger releasing to about **10-15 minutes maximum** each time, or whatever you feel is appropriate. You can do this over a period of days, weeks or months if necessary, to process and release all your hurts. Trust your instincts on this.

Some Suggested Techniques to Process Anger, or other Strong Emotions:

1- Writing it down

This is a very simple but often very effective technique to release anger.

Write the person a letter that has hurt you. Don't hold back – use strong language if appropriate and describe in detail what has caused you to have such strong feelings. Then, read this and your hurts list aloud (it can help to pretend that this person is in the room and that you are saying these things aloud to them).

Really allow yourself to **feel all of your feelings** associated with this. Then allow this other person to answer you back, using your voice, or allow them to write a letter back to you while you hold the pen, trusting that whatever they need to say to you will flow through you onto the paper. You can then read this letter aloud to yourself from this person.

You can always tear these writings up at a later date, or burn them, so that no one else needs to know your private and innermost feelings.

2- Getting Physical

In a private setting, physically process the anger out of your body – you can do this by punching pillows, using boxing gloves and a punch bag, whatever feels right to you. I sometimes even scream into a pillow, which is a wonderful way of releasing the energy associated with strong emotions. Play some loud fast music as well if you like.

You could even go to a very physical class at the gym (such as kickboxing etc.), or take part in a sports game to help release any remaining energy that is associated with these strong emotions. Punching (a pillow or punching bag) is particularly good for releasing strong emotions such as anger, resentment or rage.

3- The empty chair technique

Imagine that the other person is sitting in a chair in front of you, then go ahead and tell them exactly what you think of them and what they did that hurt you so much. Again, do not hold back here – shout and swear if you want to and do not stop until you feel satisfied that you have gotten every last hurt feeling off your chest, so to speak. Use your Hurts List from Point 3) above to help you, if needed.

4- EFT Tapping

You can also do some EFT Tapping on any strong emotions that come up for you, however with very strong emotions, such as anger or rage, I find that it is good to physically release them and say them aloud using the 3 techniques outlined above, then do some EFT Tapping on any remaining emotional charge that they have. Check your score at the beginning, then continue to tap and bring your score (ideally) to a +10 about this situation or person.

5) Look to obtain an <u>insight</u> as to why this person behaved the way that they did.

Once you feel comfortable that you have released all of the hurts that you associated with this person or situation, look to obtain an insight as to why they acted the way that they did. For instance – you could meditate, pray, ask God / a Higher Power / your Higher Self / ask your Angels for guidance -or just be still and reflect on why this happened - whatever works best for you.

In light of the above, why might this person have acted this way?

_____

_____

_____

_____

_____

"If her past was your past, her pain your pain, her level of consciousness your level of consciousness, you would think and act exactly as she does. With this realisation comes forgiveness, compassion, peace." Eckhart Tolle

It is important to note that each and every person on this planet is doing the very best that they can with what they know at any given moment. If we keep this point in mind, it can really help us to see why they acted a certain way or why they made the choices that they made in their lives (much of this may even be completely unconscious on their part).

It is worth remembering that people with low self-esteem are usually very hurt, fragile and insecure in themselves. They may come across as angry, aggressive, unkind, who bully others or they may even be the other extreme of the scale - very quiet, socially introverted, painfully shy and unsure of themself. Under the surface, they are often carrying their own pain, hurt and insecurity. This shame and unforgiveness could even be carried with them for years, maybe even decades, due to something that has happened in their past that hurt them deeply.

They may decide to heal this within themselves someday, or they may take it with them to their grave, along with their pain, hurt, bitterness and resentment. It is in fact their life and their choice whether they choose to heal from their past hurts or not.

6) See the Learning

This hurtful situation and / or this person came into your life for a reason.

What did you learn from this - about the other person? About yourself? In general?

Take some time and write down as many things as you can about the learning from this situation or person being in your life (continue on a separate page if necessary):

_____

_____

_____

_____

_____

_____

_____

_____

_____

_____

_____

_____

7) Take Appropriate Responsibility

I would encourage you to take any **appropriate responsibility** for every event that comes up in your life. Some would take it as far as to say that "you are every event that you meet", or that we "attract the partner / situation that we are ready for at that time".

For instance, if someone treated you badly over an extended period of time, perhaps you could have been more assertive with them, and / or set stronger boundaries of how you expected to be treated...? If you stayed in an unhealthy or abusive relationship for a long period of time, perhaps you could have sought out help and left earlier? Etc.

This is not about apportioning blame or making you feel bad – it is about looking at how you can grow as a person from this experience and to minimize the chances of it happening to you again - or to reduce the scale of it, should it come up again for you. It is about driving your "bus" as opposed to being a passenger on it.

I have heard it said that some people live the same year over and over again until they die. For instance, there are some people who have a really unhappy relationship that ends in a break-up, but then go on to repeat the pattern by dating or even marrying someone very similar to their ex-partner. Other people are committed to being more aware and conscious of their life choices and to grow and learn continually throughout their lives – it is these people who make a conscious effort to learn what they need to learn the first time around (or soon after) rather than repeating the same patterns over and over again in some area of their life and then wondering why they are not progressing in the way that they would like. I know which option I would choose.

How might you have contributed to this situation? What might you do differently, should a similar situation come up again?

"If your compassion does not include yourself, it is incomplete."
Gautama Buddha

8) Forgiving Yourself

Finally, is there something that you need to forgive yourself for? It may relate to this same incident, or something else entirely.

_____

_____

_____

_____

_____

_____

_____

_____

_____

_____

_____

_____

_____

_____

_____

Use this process to consciously let yourself 'off the hook' – recognize that you did your best with what you knew at the time, that you are human and that you learn from every situation in your life – the challenges and the successes alike. Remember, it is our struggles that make us stronger people and strengthens our character.

> *"The weak can never forgive. Forgiveness is the attribute of the strong."*
> *Mahatma Gandhi*

9) Declaration of Forgiveness

Once you have identified all of your hurts, processed your anger and gained an insight into why the other person acted the way that they did, it is time to make a **conscious choice** to forgive.

If you do not feel ready to proceed to the next stage, you may need to go back and do some more anger processing. Trust your instincts about this and only proceed further when you feel ready.

When you feel ***ready to forgive***, please complete, sign and date the following **declaration of forgiveness:**

Declaration of Forgiveness

I _____ (your name), now release and let go of all judgments against _____ (their name).

I forgive _____ for not being the person I would have liked him / her to be and for any and all hurts that he / she caused me, intentionally or otherwise.

I now send _____ my forgiveness. Even though I do not condone his / her actions or behaviors (and may not choose them to be part of my life now or in the future) I choose to forgive them now.

I recognize that we both did the best that we could at the time, with what we knew at that time.

I send _____ my forgiveness and I forgive myself.

I **choose** to release any anger, bitterness or resentment towards this person and in doing so, **I set myself free** and release the energy that was previously used to recall and re-experience these hurt feelings.

I am ready to heal from these past hurts at a physical, emotional, mental and spiritual level, as appropriate.

Signed: _____   **Date:** _____

---

10) Forgiveness Ritual & Ho'oponopono

You may want to combine the signing of your Declaration of Forgiveness with a brief *Forgiveness Ritual* – such as burning a candle, drinking a toast, saying goodbye to this person in your mind, saying a prayer, listening to a particular meaningful song…etc.

Again, do what feels right and what works best for you (If it does not feel right to you, then feel free to skip this ritual step from the process).

Ho'oponopono

Ho'oponopono (ho-o-pono-pono) is an ancient Hawaiian practice of forgiveness and reconciliation, with similar practices said to have been performed on some of the islands in the South Pacific. It is traditionally practiced by healing priests or "kahuna" amongst the family of someone who is physically ill.

Ihaleakala Hew Len co-authored a book with Joe Vitale called "Zero Limits", which states that the main objective (and perhaps more modern day interpretation) of ho'oponopono is getting to "the state of Zero, where we would have zero limits. No memories. No identity". To reach this state, which Len called "Self-I-Dentity", one has to repeat constantly the following mantra:

"I love you. I'm sorry. Please forgive me. Thank you."

It is based on the idea of 100% responsibility, that is to say, taking responsibility for everyone's actions (according to Vitale's interpretation), not just for one's own actions. It is an invitation for us to look within and to take responsibility for what we are contributing to and for what one is creating/manifesting in one's own life. So to change our reality, we would have to change ourselves from within, as everything exists as a projection from inside the human being.

Personally, if there are very strong emotions attached to a situation, I prefer to do the emotional release techniques as outlined in the

Forgiveness Process in this Chapter (i.e. writing it down and speaking it aloud, physically processing it such as punching pillows, using the empty chair technique, EFT tapping etc) and then to chant the Ho'oponopono mantra afterwards. This feels more authentic to me, as I will have expressed my deepest emotions first. It is then easier to enter into a state of forgiveness.

This mantra is very powerful and can be combined with EFT tapping, as demonstrated in the video on my YouTube channel – "Ingrid Darragh".

Congratulations- On completing this Forgiveness Process, on recognizing the learning and personal growth that you have achieved from having this situation and / or person come up in your life and on releasing the associated negative energy, both emotionally and physically, to make way for more positive energy and experiences to enter your life.

As you process your past hurts and the associated strong emotions, you then let go of your "story" and are able to see the learning from having this situation and / or person in your life. (Remember that everything that has happened in your life was chosen by you at a soul level before you incarnated). You are also able to take full responsibility for everything that has shown up in your life, to forgive those that you need to forgive (including yourself and God, if appropriate) and you then embody a higher level of divine love. The level of energy that you are vibrating on and radiating out into the world will increase and continue to increase. You will think, feel and act in more loving ways. When something new shows up in your life, rather than overreacting with strong emotions (I call this "reacting to everything that has ever happened to you" vs. reacting to the event / situation that you are facing in the present moment), you can respond to that one event in a more logical and appropriate way.

I highly recommend that you complete this Forgiveness Process for each of your romantic relationships, for each of your parents or care-takers that you had growing up, as well as all other close and significant relationships that you have had in your life, for instance siblings, work colleagues, etc.

By doing the work to process each and every hurt that you have experienced in your life, you are then ready to let go of and release the emotions, thoughts, feelings and energy associated with them. You then no longer need to carry them with you. You can use the full Forgiveness Process as many times as you need to, to work on each one over a period of time.

You can also do some EFT tapping on any of the remaining strong emotions, once you have processed them using the Anger Processing tips, as outlined above.

Sounds like a lot of work? Maybe it is, but believe me, it will be worth it and it is vital to do this if you are to be truly ready to connect with deeper divine love / your twin flame and to embody and radiate divine love into the world.

> *"How people treat you is their karma; how you react is yours."*
> *Dr Wayne W. Dyer*

Chapter 9

Soulmate vs. Twin Flame

"You have to keep breaking your heart until it opens." Rumi

What is a Soulmate?

We have many soulmates - these souls are within our soul family - we can have many lifetimes with them and through our relationships with them we learn, evolve and grow. This can include romantic relationships, but also siblings, parent-child relationships, friends, even special work colleagues.

As we come together over various lifetimes, it can be like gathering to perform in a play each time, with each soul family member coming together and acting out a role in this "play", which represents this lifetime. The soul that plays the cheating husband this time, may return to play the loving wife in the next lifetime, to balance out the karma between these two souls, to repay their karmic debt.

There is a deep love between soulmates and a spiritual bond that is special and unique. Our many soulmates come into our lives to help us to grow spiritually. Depending on what your soul has signed up for in this lifetime and what their soul has signed up for, you might be destined to have a very loving and happy relationship with your romantic soulmate, or you may share the kind of soulmate love that "brings in the lessons". If this is the case, then it is very likely that it will be a soulmate (rather than a twin flame) who will bring in the biggest challenges in our lives - such as: abusive behaviour, betrayal, lying, cheating, etc., or we may just grow apart after fulfilling the learning or the purpose that we have come together for, one of which could be having children together. Of course, there is vast spiritual learning and growth that will come out of these situations. It is then up to us to decide whether to remain in a relationship with that person, or if we feel that we have grown apart, then we can choose to go our separate ways and to build a new life. This type of soulmate love will bring in important lessons for our soul's growth and advancement, as opposed to a soulmate who will bring in peacefulness, contentment and even bliss – as I said, it will depend on what our soul (and theirs) has signed up to experience in this lifetime.

In her book, "The Soulmate Myth - A dream come true or your worst nightmare?", Judy Hall describes a soulmate as "A soul companion who helps us to grow....This is the person who applies a spiritual brillo pad to scour our soul to remove the encrustations of karmic and emotional patterning that have prevented us from moving into our full potential". (The term spiritual brillo pad comes from author Sue Minns who wrote "Soulmates". She had her own devastating soulmate experience, but went on to learn and grow from this and to share her wisdom and insights in her book).

My own experiences of soulmate relationships certainly "scoured my soul". One of them turned into a very emotionally abusive relationship, with a man that acted in a very emotionally immature, selfish, arrogant and judgemental way. He seemed to want his own way all of the time, was always trying to get something from me to advance himself in some way (e.g. his career) and was very uncomfortable with me doing well at anything, so he seemed to prefer it if I "stayed small', as opposed to fulfilling my potential. He had been through very traumatic experiences in his childhood and never took the time to really process and heal it all while we were together. It took me years to heal from all that happened during that relationship. At a psychic reading around that time, the reader said to me "It is as if you have been so badly hurt, that you have removed your heart, locked it in a box and put it high up on a shelf, so that no one can ever hurt you in that way ever again". I certainly felt at that time that it would be so much easier to just be on my own, than to open up to love again and learn to trust someone again. At one point, he crashed his car on purpose, with me in it (this was the car accident that led to me developing PTSD).

We finally parted ways and I began my healing journey, learning about expressing my feelings around all of this, which included deep sadness, anger and even rage at all that had occurred, before I could feel ready to forgive.

Yet another soulmate experience involved deep betrayal, where he had an affair which led to someone else becoming pregnant, as well as tens of thousands of debt being run up during our time together (all in my name) to support running two homes while he travelled and re-trained for a new job and I did my courses and qualifications. I very nearly lost my home when this relationship ended and I found myself in a position of having to sell as many of my personal possessions as I could, just to cover the bills and in the end just about managed to keep my home after I took out an IVA (Individual Voluntary agreement), an agreement to pay back what was owed over an agreed timescale whilst avoiding bankruptcy.

A few years later, I found myself in a new relationship with someone who was very spiritual. I felt so hopeful and excited about the possibilities ahead for us both - of a very deep, intimate, spiritual loving relationship, as we got engaged. However, over time, problems began to surface as he did not seem to have processed and healed all of his past hurts and he began to project onto me his deepest fears and insecurities. Another issue was that pride would surface and get in the way of him being able to have honest clear communication about things that were bothering him. As his fears would surface, these would be projected onto me, which eventually led to arguments until I needed a break and some space from it all and we eventually parted ways.

Within all of these soulmate relationships, there was often a focus on the self, where the other person wanted to put their needs first, rather than an equal partnership that took both partners' needs into account. They would also often look to me to "make them happy" or "fix" them, rather than taking responsibility for their own life and happiness and being self-accountable, as well as an unwillingness to share financial responsibility and they seemed to want to pursue their own dreams, rather than supporting my hopes and dreams as well as their own.

I remember one soulmate saying to me, "Why don't you just go and get a "proper job", rather than doing all these courses and workshops?" He did not believe in my gifts and abilities as a Healer and Writer and he certainly could not see how I could make a living doing such things. That relationship ended soon after that and I continued with my journey. Thankfully, my self-love and self-esteem had grown and increased to the extent that I did not need his approval or permission to pursue my dreams - I believed in **myself**.

One of these soulmates did not seem to support my writing aspirations. I had hoped that we could both takes turns with our career goals and aspirations, supporting each other with encouragement and with practical things that needed to be done, like cooking meals etc. However, when I mentioned that I was starting to write a book, he withdrew and focused all of his effort and attention on writing his own e-book, coming from a place of competition and ego rather than a place of love and seeing how we could mutually support each other to both finish our writing projects.

"Relationships exist to make us conscious, not happy" Eckhart Tolle

During my Life Coaching training with Coach U in the states, we were always taught to "look within". So each time these opportunities for learning presented themselves to me, I would take some time for reflection and ask myself, "What can I learn from this?" and "What do I need to do / how do I need to change & grow in relation to this?"

For instance, there was a part of me in the past that liked to "fix" people, so of course, I was going to attract someone that wanted to be fixed and coached all the time. When I was younger, I had low self-esteem, was used to putting other people's needs before my own, did not know how to express my feelings very well and was very uncomfortable with anger or conflict of any kind. So I naturally attracted partners who were used to having their needs met first in the relationship, did not know how to express their feelings and would try to control or manipulate their partner (i.e. me) with anger and aggressive behaviour.

Each time, I took responsibility for how I needed to change and grow as a person, to be ready to attract in the loving, intimate, respectful, trusting, responsible, self-aware, open-hearted, spiritual, emotionally intelligent partner that I so deeply desired. Of course, **I needed to be all of these things first**, to be an energetic match to attract this great partner into my life. This involved a great deal of personal work - of healing my past hurts, of increasing my levels of self-awareness, of being aware when I was projecting something towards another person, of when I was going into fear, rather than focusing on love, of when I was self-sabotaging myself or holding myself back in some way, of working to dissolve my ego behaviours (such as going into drama, or allowing pride to surface), of being willing to be authentic and be myself (rather than what the other person wanted or expected of me), of having good personal boundaries and being able to express these in kind and loving ways, of sharing agape love (loving without conditions or expecting something in return), of being able to deal with anger and confrontation in lovingly assertive ways, of sharing my deepest truth, even if this felt uncomfortable at times, being able to show my feelings (holding nothing back) and holding my partners hopes and dreams in my heart, making them as precious and as important as my own hopes and dreams.

"He who looks within awakens" - Jung

Going into the Furnace

It is interesting to compare our spiritual journey to that of the making of gold:

Gold in its natural state is not pure, it also contains silver or other metals

(our "impurity" can represent Ego and past hurts)

- During processing, a crusher crushes the rocks of ore which contain some of the gold, then a mill pulverises them until they have a texture similar to that of sand on the beach *(our challenges that we face in life can feel like they are crushing us and even pulverising us)*
- At another stage of processing, the gold is put into a furnace of 1,600 degrees celsius in a smelter for two and a half hours to separate the gold from the impurities *(our darkest night(s) of the soul can be likened to this stage of the process - I call it "Going into the Furnace")*
- The remaining impure mixture is tested again - if it contains any gold, it goes back into the smelter - again - until all the gold is separated *(our human form is tested again and again - and we will go through another dark night of the soul to purify us even further and to help us to release any further layers of Ego - until we become completely awakened and enlightened)*

In 2009, my father, Pat Darragh, was diagnosed with an aggressive brain tumour – I sat with him and held his hand and we talked about all that was happening. He was certainly in the equivalent of the 1,600 C smelter and he was familiar with the Going into the Furnace metaphor. I said to him "You are just going into the furnace again - and I am there with you." I had perfect faith in God's plan for him.

I have noticed in my own life and in the work that I do to support others, how often we are required to step into faith - to trust without having any substantial "proof" that things will turn out "okay". It has been at the lowest points of my life - (illness and relationship break-ups) - that I have surrendered and handed things over to God and the Angels. A big step for someone who used to like being "in charge" of things! But it was this choosing to hand things over that freed me - freed me from needing to know how things would turn out, from needing things to be how I THOUGHT they should be or how I WANTED them to be - to trusting in the Divine Plan of my life and also the lives of others.

Always remember that the darkest hour is just before the dawn.

These soulmate experiences and the lessons and learning within them were preparing me for what was to come next and without these situations, I would not have done this deep work on myself. As a direct result of these experiences, I am also in a position to support others to develop and grow in similar ways and I do 1to1 appointments and workshops to facilitate that. For all of these things, I am deeply and eternally grateful.

What is a Twin Flame?

"Twin flames, also called twin souls, are literally the other half of our soul. We each have only one twin, and generally after being split the two went their separate ways, incarnating over and over to gather human experience before coming back together. Ideally, this happens in both of their last lifetimes on the planet so they can ascend together. So you probably haven't had many lifetimes with your twin. Each twin is a complete soul, not half a soul. It is their task to become more whole, balancing their female and male sides, and ideally become

enlightened, before reuniting with their twin. This reunion is of two complete and whole beings. All other relationships through all our lives could be said to be "practice" for the twin, the ultimate relationship. A twin flame is said to be the "other half" of our soul." Antera (www.soulevolution.org)

Each twin or soul has many lessons to learn and as they learn and grow, they become more enlightened. Before we incarnate, our soul chooses the experiences that we will have in this lifetime, based on the lessons that we need to learn for our soul's progression. We also have free will, so we can choose how we react to these experiences and make choices on the other things in our lives that have not been so predetermined. As we reach the stage of enlightenment on our spiritual journey, we connect to a sense of oneness with all, we access our higher self and trust our intuition as our greatest teacher. We process and heal every past hurt, returning to harmony, peace and divine love. We transcend the ego and our greatest joy is being of divine service and supporting humanity.

Each and every relationship in our lives is an opportunity to learn and grow. Each romantic relationship in particular has important learning for us, which is preparing us for uniting with our twin again. For instance, you may have been in a relationship with a partner who was hurtful, rude or emotional or physically abusive, so that you could learn to be more assertive and to stand up for yourself more, also to have stronger boundaries. Or perhaps you fell in love with a partner and gave too much - putting them first at all times and allowing them to act in selfish ways - in this case, your lesson could have been to learn to love in a more balanced way, with the relationship being more of a partnership, with an equal and fair amount of giving and receiving within it. Every soul is on a journey and this journey will take them through many lifetimes - the ultimate lessons that we are here on this earth to learn are about love.

In her "Angel Therapy" Oracle Cards, Doreen Virtue describes a twin flame as a "romantic partner who originated from your spiritual soul group – that is, he or she is "the one"… Often, twin flames incarnate during their last lifetime on Earth – after the reincarnation cycle has been completed and all karma has been balanced."

"A twin flame is a mutually supportive, interdependent, unconditionally loving and accepting relationship between two souls with a deep connection but no karma to work on, no unfinished business to complete and no hidden agendas. They...come together to make a third entity: a relationship...they complement each other...they willingly share. They mutually respect and honour each other in their wholeness and uniqueness and they do not try to change each other although they may facilitate each other's growth. The relationship works, it does not have to be worked at....it is not perfection...but obstacles are flowed around and encompassed rather than causing discord....They come together out of pure love and for no other reason. They give each other space and support. They allow each other to be who they are and to become more of that person. Nothing is held back. There is total honesty, intimacy and trust between them and they evolve at their own pace" Judy Hall

Am I ready for / have I met my Twin Flame?

The more spiritually evolved you are at a soul level and the more that you have healed from your past hurts and transcended your ego, the more likely it is that you will connect with your twin flame in this lifetime and build a happy, compatible and sustainable relationship together.

When Twin Flames come together, it can be the most rewarding and fulfilling relationships that we can experience here on earth. Twin Flames are brought together for spiritual work. This is their main reason for coming together. They commit to coming together to help the planet and/or to help humanity in some way.

We are presently experiencing a mass awakening of human consciousness on the planet. This is allowing more Twin Flames to come together than ever before. More and more people are making a commitment to doing their personal healing work, to evolve and grow spiritually and to be ready to connect with their Twin and to fulfil their life purpose here on earth during this lifetime.

Attributes of a Twin Flame relationship vs. a Soulmate relationship

Twin Flame / divine loving relationship	Soulmate relationship that brings in lessons for our souls' growth
Pure and unconditional love that is beyond merely physical attraction	There can be conditions and a feeling of holding back (of love). Attraction is mostly physical
Deep intimacy and trust	Lack of trust. An inability or an unwillingness to acknowledge and discuss what is coming up
Both partners have done deep emotional healing on themselves	Past hurts still come up and affect the dynamics of the relationship; blaming the other for your own shortcomings / areas for development, projecting your "stuff" onto the other
A sense of ease and even bliss	Feels like hard work (even if it felt good at the start of the relationship)
Supporting and encouraging each other in all things	Competitiveness. One or both feel envious or jealous of the others gifts, talents or success; may even try to hold the other back in some way
Self-fulfilment, the other person enhances your life but is not the sole source of your happiness	An unhealthy dependency on the other person for your own sense of happiness; neediness / clinging to the other person
Openness, honesty, no hidden agendas	Power games or struggles, one person trying to control or dominate the other
A natural connectedness, regular touching, holding, affection and gentleness that leads to love making	Physical intimacy is desired or expected much more often by one of the partners than the other
Mutually beneficial, a balance of giving and receiving	One person gains much more than the other from the union / association

Both are willing to make any necessary changes to support each other and the union, such as moving location, moving in together etc.	One person is reluctant to commit fully to the relationship
Both people have processed and healed every past hurt, returning to harmony, peace, enlightenment and divine love	One person has not done as much work on themselves as the other (less self-aware, and / or past hurts have not been fully processed at a deep enough level)
Both people take full responsibility for their own thoughts, emotions and what they are attracting into their life and the energetic vibration that they are radiating into the world	One person is reluctant to take full responsibility for all their thoughts, feelings and energy and how these affect their life and those around them
Delight at the others success as their hopes and dreams come to fruition; feeling secure in one's own progress at one's own pace	Lack of support of the others hopes and dreams; feeling left out or insecure when the other pursues their own projects or interests
Deep contentment, good communication and dealing with anything that comes up right away in loving and kind ways	High levels of stress or annoyance, which eventually shows up as illness or dis-ease
Deep acceptance and appreciation of each other	Needing the other to change or be different in some way
Authenticity- a feeling of being able to be your true self	A feeling of having to be or act or behave in certain ways that do not feel natural to you
A deep sense of humility and of being of service; deeply committed to a spiritual lifestyle and life purpose	Pride and ego traits coming up, perhaps even attachment to fame and material gain
A sense of having an open heart, loving and giving to your partner from a place of pure love and joy	Keeping score, giving with an expectation of what you will get in return
One or both has a strong channel for connecting to spirit, even telepathic connection at times	

Successful or unsuccessful reunion?

Many of the twin flame reunion attempts are initially unsuccessful. This can be for various reasons.

The twin flame relationship is more intense than any other, with a deep spiritual connection. Due to this intensity, there can be no secrets between you - therefore, all of your past hurts, ego or emotional baggage will come up for healing. It is of utmost importance to work on your ego, process and heal your past hurts and to learn to be able to communicate your feelings - even those you are embarrassed about sharing, or those you feel vulnerable about - so that you can experience deep emotional intimacy with your twin and be able to communicate your feelings and express your needs in loving and kind ways.

Within a twin flame relationship, there is also a strong connection to Spirit and one or even both people will have a good channel for Spirit communication. There can even be a telepathic element to the union. Each twin's growth and awakening can be accelerated by their coming together.

In her book "Twin Flames - A story of soul reunion", Antera shares her true story of meeting and connecting with Omaran (these are their Spirit names that they have adopted), who she is told by Spirit is her Twin Flame. Antera eventually separated from her husband she was with at the time she met Omaran and they began to build a new life together. Initially blissful, over time deep unhealed pain (mostly his) is brought to the surface, which manifested as extreme aggression and even rage. This nearly caused them to separate, but they worked through it over a four year period to come to a place of great happiness, joy and even bliss.

Omaran finally did the deep emotional processing and healing work that was necessary to be with his Twin Flame. "I really think that I had a huge amount of conditioning to overcome. Way more than either of us realised. Not only the anger itself, but the programming that said 'I don't need help. I am strong. Suck it up and take it like a man. Don't complain'" and he commented that he grew up in an era where it was considered very unmanly (or perhaps even a sign of weakness) to express emotions.

Once this deep healing took place, Antera and Omaran were married and set up their non-profit Center for Soul Evolution. They also teach spiritual-growth classes and are a singer-songwriter duo, based in Mt Shasta, California (for more info on their work, please see www.soulevolution.org).

Another example of a Twin Flame relationship is outlined by Judy Hall in her book "The Soulmate Myth - A dream come true or your worst nightmare?", as she discusses the relationship between Celia Gunn (author of "A Twist in the Coyote's Tale") and her partner Anthony. Celia describes it as a feeling of coming home, a joyful and joyous connection that affords her a greater consciousness of her own Higher Self and a connection that supports them both to manifest their divine purpose - what they have come to earth to do. Celia confirms that before they came together, they each did alot of inner work to strengthen and balance their male and female energies within, to "create a sort of foundation to be able to release the Oneness".

She also talks of their first few months of being together as a couple (although they had known each other for a few years as friends prior to this) as she says "I often experienced the most extraordinary feeling of 'melting' into Anthony, even when we were just sitting together chatting. I've never felt anything like it before. It was like joining with the rest of myself that I never knew had been missing, or that I would lose myself in him, and it was a so delicious feeling...Perhaps an energy connection shared and experienced by two energetically-compatible souls?"

Anthony also shares his perspective on what it is like to be in this Twin Flame relationship "Both of us want to care for and support each other as a basic way of being together. My greatest joy is to be giving Celia her greatest joy and it is the giving which is the basis of my reward and pleasure. Fortunately, I also receive Celia's great love and concern for me at the same time, so I am nurtured as I nurture...There is no sense of envy or jealous ownership from Celia to me and vice versa...which may be a feature of all the personal work we did on ourselves in the years before we eventually met."

He goes on to say that "Twin Flames are more profound and more enduring...but it does involve (I think) alot of hard life work and preparation and it is probably more likely to occur in the second part of life than before 40 - but that is a personal opinion...Very deep down many people are really stuck in not liking themselves and wanting to stay that way."

Celia also talks about how painful it was to be away from her partner Anthony for a period of eight weeks while she was promoting her book. As Celia says, "I guess the bottom line is that each of us is primarily concerned with the other's happiness and fulfilment; and perhaps this is one of the prime indicators of the Twin Flame connection".

It is interesting to note that in both of the Twin Flame relationships I have included here, the man is significantly older than the woman – at least 10 years older, indicating that in these instances the men needed more time to cultivate a higher level of self-awareness and to process their past hurts and strong emotions, perhaps due to their conditioning, of being brought up to disconnect from and suppress their emotions, as this is often viewed as being un-manly or un-masculine.

In her book, "Love on the other side", Arielle Ford gives a beautiful example of Twin Flame connection between Richard Carlson (author of many books including "Don't Sweat the Small Stuff...and it's All Small Stuff") and his wife Kristine, who experienced a magical and very deep connection when they first met at college then went on to have 25 "magnificent years together" and two daughters. They shared many mystical experiences, including intuitive dreams, until Richards' death in 2006. Kristine felt and sensed his presence around her following his passing and also received very clear and accurate messages from a medium she connected with and says that "Love truly never dies with the body. That is what is eternal. The deeper connection you have of love in life, the deeper you experience that love forever. The only reason we are separated in form at all is ego. I know that Richard and I are twin flames".

I remember hearing a story as a young child about a young couple who fell in love and began building a life together. As they approached their first Christmas together, neither had much money to buy the other a gift. Each of them thought in turn about the others most favourite possession to help them to choose what to get each other. As she reflected on this, she thought of her husband's gold pocket watch that he so treasured. He, in turn, knew that his wife really loved her beautiful long golden hair, which was often admired by all who knew her or came into contact with her.

Christmas morning came and they embraced each other and passed on their festive wishes to each other and then the time came to exchange gifts. They were very surprised to find that he had sold his treasured pocket watch so that he could buy his wife a beautiful gold clip for her long hair. She then removed her bonnet to show that she had cut off and sold her long hair, so that she could buy him a gold chain for his pocket watch. They then had tears in their eyes as they embraced each other and shared how much they loved each other, for in truth their greatest gift was their love for each other and their presence within each other's lives.

As a child, I reflected on how wonderful it would be to love and be loved in this way, where each person held the other in such high regard and loved so deeply that the other's happiness was just as important as the person's own happiness.

Another benefit of the Twin Flame relationship is that creative energy is released and can be used for their spiritual service work, to support humanity and the planet in some way, whether that be writing music, writing books, teaching workshops, or setting up a practice to work with clients, etc.

> *"A co-committed relationship... is one in which two or more people support each other being whole, complete individuals, with each person taking 100% responsibility for his or her life...Out of this harmony, springs an enhanced energy that enables both partners to make a greater contribution than either one could have made alone."*
> Dr Gay and Dr Kathlyn Hendricks

The Hendricks talk about how they used this creative energy to raise their family, write books and teach their workshops, rather than "wasting it through conflict".

Twin souls are in effect like two faces of the same coin. It is the sacred union of the divine feminine and the divine masculine within the Self first, then the reunion, the coming together of these two emotionally mature, enlightened and balanced souls. This reunion can also be viewed as a triad, the connecting of two souls that are also connected to God/Source.

Deep connection

This twin flame connection is a very deep connection at all levels and as such it can be very overwhelming at times. There is often a telepathic aspect to the connection.

It is important to note that twin flames may or may not unite physically on the earth plane in their current lifetime. One or both may be living with another person, experiencing the lessons and growth that is necessary for them to grow and evolve spiritually. I remember the look of deep disappointment on the face of one lady who attended one of my workshops a few years back, when she realised that if she stayed with her current partner, she would not get to experience being with her twin flame in this lifetime (she was very spiritually aware and had done quite a bit of healing on herself, but her partner was not on his spiritual path - however they had young children together, so it would have broken up their family if they chose to part ways).

Not everyone is ready or willing to make the changes or go through the difficulty of separating, perhaps even divorcing, setting up a new home etc. Or one twin may be in human form and one may be in spirit form. Either way, whether twin flames connect in physical form or not, they are always connected spiritually, at a soul level.

It is also important to note that a Twin Flame connection can feel like a "soulmate" connection, if one or both partners have not yet healed their past hurts and / or if ego thoughts are coming up and are not being held in awareness and lovingly transformed. More on this in chapter 10.

Experiencing the Heart of God

I had a wonderful and very deep spiritual experience at a Healing Workshop - I have had many of these experiences over the years in classes and then on my own with the Angels and my Spirit Guides and helpers as I developed and trained as a Healer, where I experienced my heart / heart chakra opening, which then brought in a beautiful energy and feelings of bliss and even ecstasy. I would often also experience seeing or feeling or hearing my guides, angels and helpers in the spirit world, as they came close to communicate messages to me, about my life, of hope for the future, or about my life purpose and mission.

This particular experience resulted in my heart chakra opening three times, each time going deeper and opening to a new level. I actually felt a physical pain in my chest as this was happening and I was letting go of past hurts and the energy associated with them. I noticed that I felt and experienced the pain, loss and hurt about a relationship that had ended, and as part of the healing process, I allowed all of this to surface and express, so I spoke aloud the words I wanted to say and also cried the tears that needed to surface, as I moved through the hurt, disappointment, anger and sadness.

This went on for about an hour, then I felt very peaceful and I felt like I was "looking down" on the earth, as if I was above it, and the most beautiful divine loving energy flowed through me. It felt like I was connected to every single heart on the planet. Tears rolled down my cheeks as it was such an awe-inspiringly beautiful feeling of love and my entire being filled with joy, love and bliss. The only words that I can put around it was that I was experiencing the Heart of God - I felt like I was connected to the heart of every being on the planet and totally immersed in Oneness.

This went on for several minutes, then I surrendered myself fully to God's plan for me – I made a commitment to do God's work here on earth and let go of how I thought it "should be". I surrendered to this fully and at the same time I let go of every attachment that I had. It was a very intense and powerful feeling and I felt very honoured and humbled to experience it.

One of the things that resulted from this experience is the publication of this book – one of the ways that I can serve humanity and be of service to the world has been to share what I have learned with others via my writing, my blog, and my work with clients.

Our planet earth is on the verge of a great awakening. Many people are feeling a sense of this shift that is currently taking place and many are experiencing various states of enlightenment. As our physical and energetic vibrations increase, our consciousness expands and we begin to receive and accept all of who we are and why we are here on this planet at this time. An initiation of light and love occurs, which opens our Heart to deeper levels. Once you open fully to your own divine essence you can then support others with their awakening and enlightenment.

I have personally experienced very deep healing and personal transformation over the years and am honoured to be able to support others with their awakening and spiritual unfoldment.

Chapter 10

Preparing for Divine Love / Twin Flame reunion

"The purpose of a relationship is not for two incomplete people to become one,
but rather for two complete people to join together for the greater glory of God."
Marianne Williamson

As I sat down to write this final chapter, I realised that not everyone will be ready to hear or assimilate all of the content of this chapter. Or you may take it in at an intellectual or conceptual level but may not be ready yet to fully experience it – that is to say, to feel it and live it. If that is the case, I would suggest that you read it anyway and then put the book somewhere, for instance, on a book shelf or in a drawer. You can then go back to it anytime in the future. In fact, I would go so far as to say that you will be guided to lift it again when the time is right for you, when you are ready to experience the content of this chapter. We could even go a lot deeper to explore how to live and experience divine love as a way of being, as there is so much to explore and write about this – too much to confine to one chapter of one book – but hopefully this chapter will serve as a starting point for you and perhaps it may inspire your own thoughts and creative expression about this topic.

So what are some of the qualities of divine love that we can aspire to?

- A strong foundation of self-love and self-acceptance
- Good self esteem
- Has processed, healed and forgiven all hurts and wrongs
- Seeing the innocence and perfection in everyone
- Takes full responsibility for whatever is showing up in one's life
- Nurturing and nurtured
- Committed to one's own personal growth, looking for the lessons in all situations
- Tolerance - accepting oneself and others as they are
- Graciousness; celebrating all successes (as opposed to envy)
- A strong connection to God / source energy
- Complete trust in the divine plan for oneself and others
- A big, open heart, willing to show one's feelings (holding nothing back)
- Surrender to and acceptance of what is
- Living in the present moment (as opposed to dwelling on the past or worrying about the future)
- Willing to be vulnerable, emotionally intimate and to share deepest truths
- Acting with loving kindness in all situations
- Humility
- Trusting and trustworthiness
- A healthy balance of togetherness and independence
- An attitude of gratitude - grateful for all of one's blessings
- Being authentic and real
- Emotionally mature and emotionally responsible
- Lovingly assertive
- Loving without giving yourself away
- Patience
- Gentleness
- Encouraging and supportive

- Transcending Ego thinking
- Sharing agape / unconditional love - giving love without expecting something in return
- Regular spiritual practices (e.g. meditation, gratitude etc.)
- Accessing higher levels of consciousness
- A high degree of self-awareness
- Taking full accountability for everything that shows up in one's life
- Trusting and acting on one's intuition
- Knowing the difference between the head and the heart
- Committed to one's life purpose and encouraging others to fulfil theirs
- Has balanced one's own male and female energies
- Integrity; living in line with one's values
- Optimistic outlook and has a positive attitude towards life
- A sense of ease and even bliss (does not feel like it has to be "worked at")
- Deep contentment; a feeling of "coming home"
- Holding a space for each other, without needing to "fix"
- Being of service and supporting humanity and the planet
- Embodying divine love, which attracts divine love

"Ego implies unawareness. Awareness and Ego cannot co-exist." Eckhart Tolle

Transcending Ego

One of the most important prerequisites to connecting with our Twin Flame is transcending our own ego. We must develop a high degree of self-awareness and the ability to be fully present, to be aware of our thoughts and feelings in each moment and also the ability to observe our behaviours – how we are showing up in the world. In doing so, we can transcend our ego self, or "little self". We all have a voice in our head that runs in the background throughout our day - also called our "self-talk". On the most part, people are not conscious of this and this is known as the "egoic" mind - that is to say, there is a strong sense of self or "I" (ego) in these thoughts - they are self-centred. This type of thinking is also referred to as unconscious thinking. An ego thought is anything that is not coming from a place of pure love, for instance - anger, hate, resentment, blame, unforgiveness, jealousy.... etc.

However, it is important not to judge these ego-based thoughts. We may have some beliefs around some emotions being "bad" and some being "good". For instance, we may feel that it is not good to allow sadness to surface, we may feel uncomfortable about crying in front of others and feel that it is a sign of weakness to do that. We may have heard in childhood to "stop that – big girls/boys don't cry" and then we learn at school and later in the workplace that it is best to keep a stiff upper lip, as they say, and just get on with it.

Likewise, we may have been told as a child that it was naughty to have a tantrum or express anger, we may even have been punished for it, so we learned to keep any strong feelings of anger in and to ignore or supress them. Also, if someone is a very quiet and gentle person, they may be very uncomfortable with anger or conflict of any kind. If this is the case, then they will need to learn how to handle anger and conflict and how to safely and privately express it (as well as perhaps learning how to be lovingly assertive and how to have stronger personal boundaries).

These would be the two most common feelings that I see coming up for people in my private practice and at group workshops – sadness and anger. If supressed over a long period of time, these can turn into very deep resentment, depression, anxiety and even physical ailments in the body (mental, emotional or physical dis-ease).

It is important to remember that every strong feeling has a positive intention and it is vital that we allow it to surface in a safe and private way that is respectful to others. This feeling is coming up because it is ready to be looked at and released. Even jealousy, which many perceive to be a negative feeling, can have a very positive intention, it can be coming up to show us where we want to go next – as we are envious of something that the other person is doing or achieving or we want something that they have. I noticed this in my own life when I was thirty four and my older sister, Tanya, became pregnant with her second child. I really wanted to become a mother too and when she shared her news with me, I was so happy for her but I was also very jealous. Later on, I allowed these strong feelings of jealousy and envy to surface and I reflected on what they represented and what I found was that I was ready to become a mother myself and this prompted a very honest and deep discussion with my then partner and we decided to begin trying for a child of our own soon after that. In fact, my son Lewis is just five months younger than Tanya's youngest child, Eva. So in effect, taking the time to understand my feelings around all of that and to welcome the jealousy and what it was showing up to communicate to me, led to one of the greatest blessings of my life – my son, Lewis. Out of discomfort came joy, happiness and the deepest agape love, beyond anything I could ever have imagined.

Our goal is therefore not to supress or to try to stop ever having any of these ego-based thoughts, but instead we can bring awareness to them, allow them to have safe and private expression and we can welcome them with loving kindness and look for the lessons within them. We can give ourselves permission to feel all of our feelings, even if they feel uncomfortable or unpleasant. This helps us to develop emotional maturity and to take personal responsibility for whatever is showing up for us.

Another element of egoic thinking is criticism, fault finding and gossiping- at the root of this is often a desire to feel better than the person that we are complaining about. Another popular one is needing to be "right" - we may feel better and have a stronger sense of self-importance by making others "wrong".

Being attracted to drama is another egoic trait - to want to have drama in your life as opposed to peace. Take some time to notice and observe where in your life that drama is showing up for you in your life and be conscious of your reaction to this. Be curious about what you are getting out of this - do you like the extra attention? The exciting story to tell others? Or something else? By choosing to be the "observer" of what is showing up in our lives we can begin to let go of the drama and allow a peaceful resolution to the situation, to everyone's highest good, to manifest instead.

Beyond ego, you find Truth - the truth of who you are (also called the Christ Consciousness, or I Am presence; Buddhists call it your Buddha nature; Hindus call it Atman).

As you develop along your spiritual path, you can strive not to react to the ego that you are observing in yourself and others. When you can see that their behaviour is based on ego and is not personal to you and you accept this and know this to be true you can then choose to offer them love, compassion and forgiveness. You then reach a stage of knowingness that people are separate from their behaviours that they are displaying. I always find it helpful to imagine the person as a young child of about three or four years old. It is very difficult to stay angry at a child of this age, as they do not have the awareness, consciousness or emotional maturity to know what it is that they are feeling and why they are feeling it. I can then very easily and quickly open my heart to the person and focus my attention and awareness on loving thoughts and pure divine loving energy then flows through me to that person, which they can feel and often this is enough to allow the healing process to begin. People are not their behaviours. They are just acting out their pain, past hurts and supressed emotions that have not been healed yet.

> *"I (Jesus) have said 'lest you die and be born again you shall not enter the kingdom of heaven'...I was not talking about reincarnation. I was talking about the death of the ego, the death of all beliefs that separate you from others...the end of judgement...Your ego dies when you no longer have use for it" (Jesus), Paul Ferrini*

Self-awareness, Meditation and Mindfulness

One of the most powerful and effective ways that we can develop this high level of self-awareness is via meditation and mindfulness. Meditation is a holistic practice whereby we attempt to go beyond the "thinking" or "ego" mind into a deeper state of relaxation or awareness. Meditation is known to be a component of many religions, but it is also practiced outside of religious traditions.

> *"Mindfulness is an ancient Buddhist practice which has profound relevance for our present-day lives....it has... to do with waking up and living in harmony with oneself and the world...examining who we are, with questioning our view of the world and our place in it, and with cultivating some appreciation for the fullness of each moment we are alive.... Mindfulness means paying attention: on purpose, in the present moment, and nonjudgmentally." Jon Kabat-Zinn*

Mindfulness helps us to bring as much of our awareness as possible to the present moment. In doing so, we learn to live more consciously, to appreciate life and our blessings more and we learn to trust in the enfoldment of life.

Meditation can help us to achieve a heightened level of awareness and we can use meditation techniques to distance or detach ourselves from any stress, anxiety or worries of modern day living to feel more relaxed and be in a more calm and resourceful frame of mind.

It is said that during meditation, our brain waves alter:

BETA - 13-30 cycles per second - awaking awareness, extroversion, concentration, logical thinking - active conversation. So a person making a speech, or a teacher, or a talk show host would all be in beta when they are engaged in their work

ALPHA - 7-13 cycles per second - relaxation times, non-arousal, meditation, hypnosis

THETA - 4-7 cycles per second - day dreaming, dreaming, creativity, meditation

DELTA - 1.5-4 or less cycles per second - deep dreamless sleep

A good place to begin when learning about meditation is the breath. Here is an example of a simple meditation technique that I encourage my clients to practice while sitting on a chair (you can also meditate lying down, but in the beginning you are less likely to fall asleep if you are sitting upright, as your mind and your body adjusts to experiencing the brain waves associated with meditation).

You can also visit my website www.ingriddarragh.com or my Facebook page "Ingrid Darragh – Divine Love" at www.facebook.com for various video meditations, to support you to get into the regular habit of meditating. I recommend that you set aside some time to meditate every day.

Example Meditation Technique

Posture

- Sit on a straight-backed chair
- Keep your feet flat on the floor, slightly apart and in line with your shoulders
- Sit as upright as possible, with your shoulders back, (you may want to roll them back a few times to help with this)
- Place your hands on your knees, with your palms facing up or down, whichever is most comfortable for you
- Look straight ahead (keeping your head in place, i.e. do not let your chin drop too much)

Focus on your breathing by doing the following

- Inhale slowly to the count of four, allow your abdomen to expand, relax your chest and listen to your breath
- Pause for one count, then exhale slowly and completely to a count of six - with your abdomen deflating, shoulders relaxed
- Pause for one count
- Repeat this breathing exercise four more times

Relax your body

- Starting with your head and neck, then work your way down the body to the jaw, shoulders, arms, back, chest, abdomen, pelvic area, legs, ankles and feet
- Allow your consciousness to "guide" you as you slow down the mind and continue to take slow deeps breaths in and out
- If you fall asleep, that's okay (however this is more likely to happen in a lying down position and over time will happen less often as you get used to being in a meditative state)
- There will be times your meditation will be a flood of imagery, sounds and/or sensations. On other occasions, you may see, hear or feel nothing
- Just trust that whatever happens each time you meditate is exactly what is supposed to happen at that time

Let go of any thoughts that come to you

- When thoughts come into your mind / consciousness, just bring your focus and attention back to your breath
- You could choose to repeat a mantra - e.g. repeating a word such as "Love", "Health", "Wellness", "Peace"
- Or you could try chanting "Omm" over and over again
- Continue to do this for at least 2 minutes, then over time, build this up to 15 minutes, then 30 mins and then eventually even 1 hour at a time

- When you are ready, bring your attention back into the room where you are sitting, feel your feet on the floor, have a little stretch and open your eyes.

You may want to play some soft relaxing music in the background to add to the experience, or you may prefer the stillness that silence brings.

Anyone can learn the art of meditation. I myself went from a busy person working in the corporate world, who hardly ever sat still for any length of time, to becoming someone who now meditates every day, teaches others how to meditate and is a Reiki Master Teacher.

"Mastery of your own thoughts is essential for your enlightenment. For it is in your thoughts that you choose to walk with me or to walk away from me" (Jesus), Paul Ferrini

Be still and know

By slowing down, sitting in silence more often, and incorporating meditation and stillness into our day to day lives, we can choose to be less reactive to the things that are going on around us and we can choose how we respond to these things that are showing up in our lives. In time, these new habits and practices become a way of life for us, a natural state of being, where we can listen to our inner voice, that part of us that knows all there is to know, that accesses universal wisdom and transcends ego thoughts and the egoic mind. We can then learn to witness the ego or little self – to be aware of in the present moment - those thoughts, actions and behaviours that are grounded in anything that does not stem from love (e.g. separation, fear, guilt, lack, unworthiness etc.) and we can then meet these thoughts with love, acceptance, kindness and compassion, as we grow towards enlightenment.

Having practiced this in my own life for many years now, I regularly flow between these two states of my ego self and my divine or higher self. I notice that my ego self has much less power now and I am more often than not able to "catch" my ego thoughts and actions quickly as they arise and then make a conscious choice towards something else. By that I mean, I will -

- Take some time out to **observe** whatever is coming up
- **Process** whatever it is that comes up (sadness, anger etc.)
- **Allow** this to express and have a voice
- **Look for the lessons** within this situation
- **Take responsibility** for it
- **Share my truth** with loving kindness about this situation, as appropriate
- Communicate my **personal boundaries** (and review these, if necessary)
- Be **gentle and loving** with myself as I grow and evolve as a result of this situation

> *"Enlightenment is the moment when you let the fearful, separate ego state fall away altogether"* Miranda Macpherson

Higher consciousness

Higher consciousness is generally regarded as a state of consciousness in which attention is improved, refined and enhanced and aspects of the mind (such as thought, and perception) are transcended. This can be cultivated by greater control over one's mind and profound personal growth and can lead to spiritual enlightenment and union with the divine.

Christ Consciousness

Christ consciousness is the direct line to God / source / the divine. Many of the Masters that have walked this earth (including Jesus, Buddha and many others) chose to walk in peace, becoming enlightened on their journey. We all have this energy within us - we can choose love over fear. We can cultivate this consciousness to a deeper level through prayer, meditation, choosing love and kindness, forgiving all hurts, transcending Ego thinking, connecting with Oneness and returning to your true self.

Healing every past hurt

"When you ask God to heal your life, He shines a very bright light on everything you need to look at. You end up seeing things about yourself that maybe you'd rather not see...the process of personal growth is not always easy...It often seems, in fact, that our lives get worse rather than better when we begin to work deeply on ourselves. This process can be so painful that we are tempted to go backwards. It takes courage - this is often called the path of the spiritual warrior - to endure the sharp pains of self-discovery rather than choose to take the dull pain of unconsciousness that would last the rest of our lives" Marianne Williamson

In order to be ready to come together with our Twin Flame, it is so important to process and heal every past hurt. You can use the techniques outlined in chapter 8 on how to process strong emotions and use the forgiveness process to support you to do this deep level of healing on yourself. You can also use EFT tapping and any other techniques that you have come across that you find helpful.

If you do not take the time to do this at a deep enough level, these hurts will eventually surface and it may lead to one or both of you withdrawing from each other and you will be very likely to "project" your hurts onto each other. Projection is when you blame or "attribute to another person something that is actually going on at an unconscious level within yourself" (Dr Gay & Dr Kathlyn Hendricks). In other words, it is so important that you take ownership for your own "stuff" that comes up, rather than blaming or pointing the finger at your partner.

"What hurts you, blesses you... The cure for pain is in the pain." Rumi

Authenticity

The Hendricks also talk in their book about telling what they call the microscopic truth - "this is when you speak the truth about your internal experience as you are currently perceiving it". It is vital to make a commitment to share your deepest truth with your partner, even if it feels uncomfortable. So if you are experiencing strong feelings, for instance fear of any kind, you would sit down and discuss this with your partner, as opposed to covering it up and pretending it did not exist and hoping that it would go away. If we do not share and communicate our truth, it can be like repeatedly sweeping dirt under a rug and over a period of time there is then a huge pile of dirt under the rug, which can then explode into a nasty argument. The energy of this suppressed emotion could also be felt by your sensitive partner. It is much more effective to deal with things as and when they come up.

To embody divine love, it is so important to be authentic and real with each other, which means being prepared to remove the "masks" that we often wear in the presence of others. We must be willing to be vulnerable, to share our deepest fears and past hurts with each other, to be met with acceptance, understanding, loving kindness, compassion and unconditional love.

Loving without giving yourself away

It is also important to cultivate a healthy balance of closeness and independence, to have a strong sense of self and pursue your own hopes and dreams and creative expression in the world, while also having a deep connection with your partner.

This means making sure that you are aware of your own needs and how to get these met and acknowledging that your needs are just as important as the needs of your partner. Otherwise, an unhealthy co-dependency can develop, where one partner is dependent on the needs of/or control of another person. One partner may puts their needs below the other partner's due to their low sense of self-esteem and self-worth. A codependent person will take responsibility for their partner, for their feelings, their happiness, their problems, rather than trusting them to deal with their own feelings and their own issues that come up in their life.

In her book "Codependent no more", Melody Beattie shares an example of a lady called Kristen who is married with two children. Kristen describes herself as codependent in that she tries to control the feelings of others and she also allows other people's moods to control her emotions. She says:

"If my husband is happy, and I feel responsible for that, then I am happy. If he's upset, then I feel responsible for that too. I'm anxious, uncomfortable, and upset until he feels better. I try to *make* him feel better. I feel guilty if I can't. And he gets angry with me for trying.... Somehow, I just seem to lose myself in other people".

Beattie defines a codependent as being "someone who has let another person's behaviour affect him or her, and who is obsessed with controlling that person's behaviour". They often like to be and need to be needed and like to be the "fixer" in a relationship.

In order to love someone as an equal, without giving yourself away, it is important to see your partner as an adult, as someone who is fully in charge and responsible for sorting out their own life. How are they going to grow as a person and learn the lessons that they are destined to learn if you just jump in and rescue them every time that something challenging presents itself? You would in fact be doing them a disservice by doing that. It is therefore necessary to be aware of any codependent behaviours in your relationship (yours or your partners) and to bring awareness to these so that they can be healed and a more equal partnership can then be established, where both partners' needs are respected and honoured as being of equal importance.

Balancing your male and female energies

We all embody male and female energy within us, regardless of our gender. Typically, masculine energy is more assertive, goal-oriented, analytical, impatient, competitive etc, whereas feminine energy is softer, nurturing, gentler, more intuitive and patient.

It is important to be aware of and be willing to balance these energies within oneself, as too much dominance of one over the other causes problems for the individual. It is only when we have balanced these masculine and feminine aspects that we come into harmony within ourselves. Many of the clients that I work with are out of balance and we then look at this together. I personally was also out of balance at one stage of my life when I was working in the corporate world. My masculine energy was dominant, as I needed to be analytical, logical, aggressive and focused on achieving the goals that were set by the management team. To exist in and operate effectively in that male-dominated environment I supressed my femininity - my softer, gentler side. I very much enjoyed exploring my femininity and allowing it to manifest more fully when I became a mother and also as a healer, in fact many people have commented on the divine feminine energy being with me very strongly. I am now more balanced – I can still focus on my goals and can be assertive when I need to, as well as being a loving, caring, kind, gentle and (sometimes) vulnerable woman.

I remember when I was in a relationship with my son's father when I was in my early-thirties and was going through a divorce and recovering from the pituitary illness and PTSD. I would sometimes be very tired when we had arranged a date and I had to discuss this with him when we started dating, so that he knew that this could potentially come up. Also, I was not able to work at that time due to my health issues, so I also told him about that. I was aware that I did not have some of the usual things that some people look for in a potential partner, such as earning power and vitality. I remember feeling nervous about whether he would still want to be with me. I was worried that he may judge me or see me as weak or inferior because of this. All I had to offer him was myself. I felt very vulnerable and uncomfortable, especially as I had previous had a "successful" career, a good salary and good health. Similarly, he had ended a previous relationship and moved to Belfast and was renting an apartment and did not have a car yet. All he had to offer me was himself. My fears were unfounded however, as we fell completely in love with each other.

This was my first real experience of unconditional love and acceptance within a relationship. I remember feeling overwhelmed at the time and if I am completely honest, I felt like running away at times! But my self-awareness was increasing all the time and I was able to look at what I was feeling and realise what was happening. The gift in all of this was that I gave myself permission to be vulnerable (more feminine), to show up as I am and to trust that it was enough. It turned out that the love that we shared was the soulmate love that brings in lessons and we grew apart over time, but this beautiful gift has stayed with me.

Some of the women that I work with are very much in touch with their feminine side but have not developed their masculine energies to be able to access their assertiveness, their personal power and being able to stand up for themselves, to deal with anger and/or conflict and to be able to communicate their personal boundaries with others. Again, this is something that can be developed and learned so that it becomes a part of who you are. You can still be a kind, gentle and loving person, but can access your assertive side as and when it is required.

In her book "Powerful and Feminine" Rachael Jayne Groover gives many wonderful examples of exercises for women to learn about how they can embody more of their feminine essence and personal presence, to embrace vulnerability and to live with an open heart.

It is important to note that I have also come across men who have an imbalance of male energy and they then need to address this by learning to become more patient, nurturing, emotionally intelligent, compassionate etc. and be able to communicate their feelings and allow themselves to be vulnerable. At the other extreme, some men's feminine energy is too dominant and they can then look at developing their masculinity.

The Crisis

Once Twin Flames connect and come together, the magic and excitement of this can fade somewhat over time and the reality of day to day life can settle in and the Ego or little self can resurface. Conflicts can occur at this time and doubts can surface. However, this is all part of coming together and these issues are actually coming to the surface to be healed.

This can feel very uncomfortable or even painful and some people may choose to give up or to walk away from the relationship at this time, or they may not know how to deal with whatever is coming up. Antera and Omeran experienced this stage in their relationship, as outlined in "Twin Flames - a story of soul reunion". They worked through the deep levels of pain from Omeran's past, so that he could take responsibility for and process the pain that would manifest and show up as anger and sometimes even rage. He learned how to express and process and release everything from his past that was associated with this, as well as how to take time out to deal with anything new that may come up that could trigger these strong feelings.

This pain, if very intense, may lead to withdrawal or a break-up of the relationship. It is <u>vital</u> to get support if you are not sure how to work through these old behaviours and patterns. It is so important to be patient and compassionate as you and your partner each allow your hurts to surface for healing. These may be very old and very deep wounds, which will need love, kindness and gentleness as they heal.

It is only through allowing and processing these deep hurts that Twin Souls can come together fully. Each must also transcend their ego and strengthen their connection with God/source. One Twin may need to be more patient and allowing of the space and time for their partner to reach this stage, or they may take turns to support each other as and when something comes up that needs to be healed. Each Twin can offer support and patience and love while their partner becomes more awakened and enlightened.

The Awakening

As the ego layers dissolve and melt away, there is a greater opportunity for each Twin to embrace their divinity and to fully awaken spiritually. This can happen in stages, with various ego traits being released and dissolved, or it can be more dramatic and happen all at once. We then radiate divine love outwards, into the world.

Once both Twins have fully awakened, their union deepens and this deep spiritual connection is a foundation for their spiritual work here on earth and they can then assist others with their heart opening and their awakening.

> *"If you want to be like me, I will help you, knowing we*
> *are alike. If you want to be different, I will wait until you*
> *change your mind" (Jesus) - A Course in Miracles*

Exercise - Divine Loving Relationship Values

Imagine that you are standing at an altar / or at a commitment ceremony with your **twin flame / divine loving partner** - about to make a lifetime commitment with the person standing opposite you - this amazing partner that you have designed, attracted and manifested into your life, that is beyond your wildest dreams.

What do you need this relationship to have or embody - for you to feel confident and comfortable with making that lifetime commitment?

For instance: acceptance, trust, respect, tenderness, gratitude, emotional honesty, spirituality, compassion, fun, peace, unconditional love, kindness, ease, intimacy, self-love, nurturing, emotional intelligence, gentleness, generosity, patience, sensitivity, freedom, loyalty, responsibility, energetic connection, romance, self-awareness…etc.

Here is my list of divine loving relationship values. Doing this exercise really helped me to become clear on what was most important to me in my new relationship that I was seeking. Once I became completely clear, I was then able to focus my attention on it to help to manifest it in my life.

My divine loving relationship values

Divine love – divine love fills my being and is a foundation for all aspects of our life together

Integrity – a strong sense of integrity and values underpins who we are and all that we do

Tenderness – my life is full of tender moments and I love how this feels, both physically and emotionally

Appreciation – I am appreciated fully and I appreciate fully

Kindness – kindness and consideration are key priorities and a natural way of being for us

Passion – my partner and I demonstrate our love for each other regularly and in ways that bring us both great pleasure

Acceptance – I am loved completely for who I am and I love completely who my partner is

Fun & laughter – I laugh every day, seeing the lightness in all situations and interactions with people

Peace – we live in peace, ease and harmony and we deal with anything that comes up in a timely and loving way to come back to peace as soon as reasonably possible

Compassion – my partner and I love each other with big open hearts, understanding who we each are, with tenderness and loving kindness

Take some time to reflect on what your divine loving relationship values are. They will be unique to you and will reflect what is most important to you. Indeed, they may change over time as you continue to learn and grow, so you can review them periodically to ensure that they are an up to date reflection for you.

_____

_____

_____

_____

_____

_____

_____

_____

_____

_____

Metta bhavana (the cultivation of loving kindness)

One of the most beautiful practices that I have come across to support the shift of the focus from the Self (ego) towards Oneness is Metta – this is the cultivation of loving kindness, a popular form of meditation in Buddhism. The practice begins with cultivating loving-kindness towards oneself, then one's loved ones, friends, teachers, strangers, enemies and finally towards all sentient beings.

The original name is *metta bhavana*, (which comes from the Pali language). The most common form of the practice is as follows and each stage should last about 5 minutes when you are beginning the practice. You can do this regularly, in fact it is a wonderful practice to do daily.

Exercise – the practice of metta (cultivating loving kindness)

1 Begin by sitting comfortably and taking a few deep breaths to calm and center yourself.

2 Feel loving kindness (metta) for yourself – focus on feelings of love, kindness, compassion, peace and calm towards yourself. Allow these to grow and to develop into feelings of love in your spiritual heart center (the middle of your chest). Say aloud "May I be well and happy". Envisage a golden light filling your body.

3 Focus on loving kindness for a good friend – bring them to mind and focus on their good qualities, the things that you like and admire about them. Say aloud "May you be well and happy" and envisage the golden light flowing from your heart center to theirs.

4 Bring to mind someone that you feel neutral about that you may not know that well – whom you neither like nor dislike. Reflect on them and see their innate goodness and their humanity. Say aloud "May you be well and happy" and envisage the golden light flowing from your heart to theirs.

5 Bring to mind someone that you dislike. Connect with their humanity. Say aloud "May you be well and happy" and envisage the golden light flowing from your heart to theirs.

6 Finally, think of all four people – yourself, your friend, the person you feel neutral about and the one you dislike. Then, extend your feelings of loving kindness further – to everyone around you, the area where you live, your town, your country, then allow this to spread throughout the world. Feel these waves of loving kindness and the golden light spreading from your heart to everyone, to all beings everywhere.

7 Gradually relax out of the meditation and bring your attention back into the room to conclude your practice of Metta.

Oneness

I will conclude by sharing with you a message from my guides and helpers in the spirit world:

Separateness is an illusion, orchestrated by the ego. The ego purports this myth and the majority of mankind are too busy and too occupied with day to day living to question this.

Do you really think that you are here on this earth at this time to acquire "things"? This notion is quite preposterous. But still, many engage in the busy-ness, the doing, the achieving, the striving, and the seeking.

Transformation is taking place on earth at an alarming rate, more so than ever before. There are vast opportunities for spiritual growth and enlightenment. These opportunities are available to all, but not everyone is ready or indeed willing to seize them. Many are still engaged in progressing the goals of the self, of acquiring, doing, completing, achieving. This is not the way of our father.

See through the eyes of perfect love. As you gaze from your eyes into the eyes of your brother, you connect with the essence of your own soul. As you look from this vantage point of the purest of love (that is to say, that which is without ego), you will see that he is in fact you and you him. Divine interconnectedness is a state of being that we all have access to. All we need to do is be willing to open up to it. It is indeed our divine inheritance.

If you could see but for a moment the beauty and the potential within even a fraction of your soul, you would be breathlessly captivated for all eternity.

As you reconnect with your own divinity, you remember who you are and why you are here on this planet at this time. You are here to experience and learn about love. Love one another as I have loved you.

Do not point your finger at your brother when he is only holding a mirror up for you to gaze into. Instead, use this mirror as a tool to look within, yes, even to the depths of your own soul. What lurks here that needs your attention, your patience and your love, that you can return again to the essence of who you are? Put your attention there.

Just as a lion tamer works to tame the wild animal, the so-called king of the beasts, so you must learn to tame that which is called the ego. For when you are distracted, it will rise up and attack without warning. It is only when you have learned to anticipate its every thought, its every move, that you can pre-empt its next strike. Then and only then will it lose its power. Then and only then will you be in control.

Many of you that have requested to experience fully the capacity for divine love will first of all experience the deepest hurts that are possible in this existence. It is in experiencing and feeling these degrees of hurt and pain that your heart will open to the deepest possible levels and you will connect to the depths of your soul, where ego layers dissolve and fall away. For it is this place (and only this place) from which divine love can be felt and experienced (in human form).

If you are reading this and realising that you are with a "soulmate", do not despair. Sometimes you will need to be with the one before "the one", so that when "the one" does come into your life, you will appreciate all of their qualities, who they are as a person and all of the ways that you will enhance each other's lives. It is this very <u>contrast</u> *that will deliver knowingness beyond any shadow of a doubt and you will then experience divine love in its fullest glory.*

Do not underestimate what will be required of you in order for you to connect with and live in harmony and eventual bliss with your Twin Flame – it is certainly not for the weak, the fainthearted or the uncommitted. However, it is possible, for those who are willing to put in the effort that is required to lay the necessary foundations for this soul reunion.

A soulmate cannot give to you what he does not possess in himself or for himself. What can happen here is that he will try to open up his heart to divine love, however, the intensity of this can leave him feeling completely overwhelmed (and unable to deal with the intensity), so he will choose instead to shut down, to close his heart, to distract, to delay, to blame, to fear... In effect, he will be unable to hold the energetic vibration within his energy field that accompanies the twin flame energy. He will eventually be exhausted from his efforts, as will you. It would be far better to release him from your sights and in doing so, free him to connect with another that is an energetic match to his, whilst being mindful and appreciative of the lessons that he brought into your life, knowing these to be the most precious of gifts to you at a soul level.

As you do your inner work to prepare to connect with your Twin, it may feel like a lonely path at times, but know that once you are both ready, you will connect with the highest form of love possible on this planet and your eventual rewards will more than exceed your efforts that you put in. This process is unlikely to be a smooth one, an easy option or be achieved in a short timescale, but for those that are willing to undertake it and see it through to completion the rewards will be immeasurable and will defy even your wildest imaginings and your deepest longings.

By all means, spend time supporting each other through the process of opening and awakening, but be aware when external support is required and make a commitment to finding the necessary teachers and helpers along the way. This will save you much heartache, suffering and pain.

We watch your development, your soul's growth and expansion. Just as children fall over as they learn to walk, you will stumble and fall on many occasions along the way. The key to your progress is to persevere. Rest at times if you must, but always persevere. Your reward will be to experience heaven here on earth.

I wish you every blessing on your journey to experience and connect with divine love of the self, with healing and forgiving every past hurt, learning the necessary lessons from your soulmate relationship(s), transforming the ego, connecting with your twin flame and embodying and radiating divine love into the world, for this is indeed your divine inheritance.

May all beings be blessed, content, happy and at peace.

Gandhi's Prayer for Peace:
I offer you peace.
I offer you love.
I offer you friendship.
I see your beauty.
I hear your need.
I feel your feelings.
My wisdom flows from the Highest Source.
I salute that Source in you.
Let us work together for unity and love.

Recommended reading & resources

"A Course in Miracles", Foundation of Inner Peace, (Viking Penguin, 1996)

"The Wisdom of Florence Scovel Shinn", Florence Scovel Shinn, (Fireside, Simon & Schuster, 1989)

"Practicing The Power of Now", Eckhart Tolle, (New World Library, 1999)

"Boundless Love – Transforming your life with grace and inspiration", Miranda Macpherson (formerly Holden), (Rider, 2002)

"Energy EFT", Dr S Hartman, (Dragon Rising Publishing, 2012)

"The Tapping Solution", Nick Ortner, (Hay House, 2013)

"Conscious Loving - the journey to co-commitment", Dr Gay & Dr Kathlyn Hendricks, (Bantam, 1992)

"You Can Heal Your Life", Louise L Hay, (Hay House, 1999)

"For one more day", Mitch Albom, (Sphere, 2007)

"Love without Conditions - Reflections of the Christ Mind", Paul Ferrini, (Heartways Press, 1994)

"The language of letting go", Melody Beattie, (Hazelden Meditation Series, 1990)

"A return to love – reflections on the principles of "A Course in Miracles", Marianne Williamson, (Thorsons, 1996)

"Powerful and Feminine", Rachael Jayne Groover, (Deep Pacific Press, 2011)

"The Secret" - Rhonda Byrne, (Simon & Schuster Ltd, 2006)

"The Law of Attraction – How to make it work for you", Esther and Jerry Hicks, (Hay House, 2006)

"The Soulmate Secret - Manifest the love of your life with the law of attraction", Arielle Ford, (Harpercollins, 2011)

"Collins English Dictionary", (Harpercollins, 2005)

"Stillness Speaks", Eckhart Tolle, (Hodder Mobius, 2003)

"Zero Limits", Joe Vitale & Ihaleakala Hew Len (John Wiley & Sons, 2009)

"Angel Therapy" Oracle Cards, Doreen Virtue, (Hay House, 2008)

"The Soulmate Myth - a dream come true or your worst nightmare?", Judy Hall, (Flying Horse Books, 2010)

"Love on the Other Side: Heavenly help for love and life", Arielle Ford, (CreateSpace, 2014)

"Soulmates", Sue Minns, (Hodder Mobius, 2004)

"Twin Flames - a story of soul reunion", Antera, (Twinsong press, 2003)

"A Twist in the Coyote's Tale", Celia Gunn, (Archive Publishings, 2006)

"A New Earth", Eckhart Tolle, (Penguin, 2005)

"Wherever You Go, There You Are - Mindfulness Meditation for Everyday Life", Jon Kabat-Zinn, (Piatkus Books, 1994)

"Codependent no more", Melody Beattie, (Hezelden Foundation, 1987)

About the Author

Ingrid Darragh worked in the corporate world as a project manager for ten years, then experienced several challenges in her personal life, including: a divorce, a serious illness (when she was diagnosed with a pituitary tumour) and also extreme PTSD (Post traumatic stress disorder). In the years that followed, she also faced financial ruin and life as a single parent.

She chose to look for the learning and to see the blessings in the events that showed up in her life and retrained as a Spiritual Life Coach, Master EFT Practitioner, Reiki Master Teacher & Psychic Medium. She now dedicates her life to supporting others through their greatest challenges and runs her private practice in Belfast, Northern Ireland, in the UK, as well as working with clients from all over the world via Skype and Teleclasses.

In this, her first book, *"Divine Love - from Soulmate Lessons to Twin Flame Reunion"*, Ingrid shares proven techniques to support you to:

- Boost your levels of self-love, by falling in love with yourself
- Become clear about what it is that you are looking for in a partner
- The importance of forgiveness and healing every past hurt

- Use the law of attraction and gratitude to help manifest divine love in your life
- Deal with anything that is blocking you from allowing divine love into your life
- Understand the difference between a soulmate connection and a twin flame relationship
- Learn how to embody the attributes of divine love and be ready to connect with your twin flame

Based on many years of coaching clients on a 1to1 basis and in group workshops, this book is filled with real life case studies and the valuable lessons inherent within them, as well as Ingrid's own life experience, backed up by practical life coaching exercises and EFT tapping that you can do to attract the love that you deserve.

Whether you wish to improve upon an existing relationship or attract a new partner, this book has valuable insights to support you to attract higher levels of **divine love** into your life.... starting today!

For more information about Ingrid's work, her workshops & events and supporting materials (including video blog) please see: *www.ingriddarragh.com*

Printed in the United States
By Bookmasters